POTTER v. SHRACKLE AND
THE SHRACKLE CONSTRUCTION COMPANY

Problems and Case File

NITA Educational Services Committee
1996

POTTER v. SHRACKLE AND
THE SHRACKLE CONSTRUCTION COMPANY

Problems and Case File

by

Kenneth S. Broun
Professor of Law
University of North Carolina

and

James H. Seckinger
Professor of Law
University of Notre Dame

REVISED FOURTH EDITION
1992

Broun and Seckinger, *Potter v. Shrackle and The Shrackle Construction Company Problems and Case File* (Revised Fourth Edition, 1992).

ISBN: 1-55681-313-9

6/96

SECTION I

PROBLEMS

POTTER v. SHRACKLE AND
THE SHRACKLE CONSTRUCTION COMPANY

TABLE OF CONTENTS

INTRODUCTION

The problems in this book are intended to simulate realistic courtroom situations. Advance preparation is essential to their successful utilization as instructional materials.

These problems refer to *Potter v. Shrackle and the Shrackle Construction Company*, one of the case files in NITA's *Problems and Cases in Trial Advocacy*, Law School Edition, series. These case files have been designed to simulate the materials a trial lawyer would have on the eve of trial. The materials must be mastered before attempting to perform the problems in a courtroom setting.

All years in these materials are stated in the following form:

- ■ YR-0 indicates the actual year in which the case is being tried (i.e., the present year);
- ■ YR-1 indicates the next preceding year (please use the actual year);
- ■ YR-2 indicates the second preceding year (please use the actual year); etc.

At the outset we should acknowledge that it is impossible for one person to teach another how to become a trial lawyer. Advocacy is an art, the performance of which is dependent on talent and mastery of skills. One becomes a trial lawyer through a mixture of predisposition, motivation, observation, doing it, reading how others have done it and then constantly repeating the latter three — doing, observing, and reading.

It is possible, however, to simulate some of the intellectual, ethical, emotional, and physical demands of trial lawyering and advocacy teaching in a mock courtroom or classroom setting. That is what is done at the National Institute for Trial Advocacy. These materials are intended to serve as the basic teaching materials for trial advocacy courses and programs that are based upon the learning-by-doing method. Although the materials have been prepared especially for NITA programs, they are adaptable for use in other settings.

Most of the skills learned in a trial advocacy course will be applicable to trial work generally, without regard to the nature of the case. Obviously, however, different kinds of cases present different problems. We believe that these materials illustrate some of the more significant peculiarities of fire insurance contract litigation.

The student should read the assigned case file as soon as possible. A reading of the complete case file early will permit the student to fit an individual problem into the context of the entire litigation. The student should then read the assigned problems and do as much preparation as possible in advance of the program. Preparation time during the program will be limited. Thus, advance preparation will allow a more efficient use of the limited time available during the program.

METHOD OF INSTRUCTION

NITA programs, and other learning-by-doing programs, have certain unique characteristics to which these materials are particularly suited. These programs typically use teaching teams comprised of law teachers, practicing trial lawyers, and judges. The programs are highly intensive, all-day sessions lasting from five to sixteen working days. All make substantial use of videotape to record student performances for later playback and critique.

These materials also are adaptable for the more typical law school program in which classes are spread out over a semester, teaching teams are unavailable, and videotape may not be feasible. The following are some ideas for use of the materials whether they are used at an intensive NITA-type session or in a longer law school program.

It is contemplated that the materials will be used in a simulated courtroom session. A judge, whether actual or portrayed, will preside at the front of the classroom. A student lawyer will be called on to begin the problem. The examining lawyer will be opposed by an adversary, who will be portrayed by another member of the class or, when a teaching team is available, by a visiting lawyer. The witness will have been prepared and will respond to a proper examination. The lawyer may complete the examination or be interrupted so that another lawyer can continue the examination. Several lawyers may be called on to represent both sides before the problem is exhausted and the next problem begun.

At a NITA session, a section of twenty-four students will remain together for two hours to work on a series of problems. The section then ordinarily will split into two or three smaller groups. The students will continue to work on the problems in these groups.
During the course of any presentation by a student, whether in large or small groups, another lawyer may be called on to substitute for the participating lawyer. The substituting lawyer may pick up where the other left off or, with permission of the instructor, may begin again. In short, the students may be called on at any time to undertake an assigned examination.

Many teachers require universal preparation; each student must be prepared to perform at least one side of each problem.

DIRECT, CROSS, AND REDIRECT EXAMINATION

The ability to examine and oppose the examination of witnesses in open court in an adversary setting is the most basic skill of the trial lawyer. Yet, the most common criticism of trial lawyers is that they are unable to conduct proper, intelligent, and purposeful examinations and to oppose these examinations.

As with any skill, practice is the only sure way to achievement. The practice should be conducted with some guidelines in mind.

1. The purpose of any witness examination is to elicit information.

2. The basic format is an interrogative dialogue.

3. The witness is probably insecure. She is appearing in a strange environment and is expected to perform under strange rules. This is a handicap you must overcome on direct and an advantage you have (and may choose to exploit) on cross.

4. Your questions should be short, simple, and understandable to the witness, the judge, and the jury on both direct and cross examination.

    (a) It is imperative that your audience — the judge and the jury — understand your question so that they can reasonably anticipate and comprehend the answer.

    (b) On direct examination, the insecurity or anxieties of the witness will be increased if he does not understand your questions.

    (c) On cross examination, the complex argumentative question provides a refuge for the witness to evade the point.

5. As a general proposition, you may not lead on direct except as to preliminary matters or to refresh the recollection of the witness. Both of these exceptions are discretionary with the judge.

6. In any event, on direct examination leading questions and the perfunctory answers they elicit are not persuasive.

7. On cross examination you may lead and you should do so. Control of the witness on cross is imperative.

8. At the outset of direct examination, have the witness introduce herself. Then, place her in the controversy on trial, and elicit the "who, where, when, what, how, and why" of the relevant information the witness has to offer. Then quit. Do not be repetitious.

9.   If you know that the cross examination will elicit unfavorable information, consider the possible advantage of eliciting it during your direct examination.

10. Do not conduct a cross examination that does nothing other than afford the witness an opportunity to repeat his direct testimony.

   (a)   If there is nothing to be gained by cross examination, waive it.

   (b)   If you can accomplish something by cross examination, get to it. Organize your points and make them.

   (c)   Be cautious about cross examining on testimony elicited on direct that was favorable to your position. You may lose it.

   (d)   Be cautious about asking questions to which you do not know or cannot reasonably anticipate the answer. Be particularly cautious in these situations if the only evidence on the point will be the unknown answer.

11. Listen to (do not assume) the answers of the witness. As an examiner, you are entitled to responsive answers. Insist on them by a gentle repetitive question on direct or a motion to strike on cross. Of course, if the answer is favorable, accept it and return to the pending question.

12. Objections to the form of the question must be made before an answer is given. If the question reveals that the answer sought will be inadmissible, an objection must precede the answer. The grounds of the objection should be succinctly and specifically stated. If the question does not reveal the potential inadmissibility of the answer, but the answer is inadmissible, a prompt motion to strike should be succinctly and specifically stated. Only the interrogator is entitled to move to strike an answer on the *sole* ground that it was unresponsive to the question. If the answer is unresponsive *and* contains objectionable matter, then the opposing counsel is entitled to object.

13. If an objection to the content of the answer (e.g., relevancy, hearsay, etc.) as opposed to the form of the question, is sustained, then the interrogator should consider the need for an offer of proof at the first available opportunity. If an objection to the form of the question is sustained, then the interrogator should rephrase the question to cure the objection.

PROBLEM 1

Marilyn Kelly

Assume that the case is at trial and the plaintiff's first witness was Officer Young. The plaintiff's next witness is Marilyn Kelly.

(a) For the plaintiff, conduct a direct examination of Mrs. Kelly.

(b) For the defendants, conduct a cross examination of Mrs. Kelly.

(c) For the plaintiff, conduct any necessary redirect examination.

PROBLEM 2

Charles Shrackle

Assume that the case is at trial, the plaintiff has presented his case, and the defendants' motion for a directed verdict has been denied. The defendants' first witness is Charles Shrackle.

(a) For the defendants, conduct a direct examination of Mr. Shrackle.

(b) For the plaintiff, conduct a cross examination of Mr. Shrackle.

(c) For the defendants, conduct any necessary redirect examination.

HANDLING AND INTRODUCTION OF EXHIBITS

The ability to examine and oppose the examination of witnesses in open court in an adversarial setting is the *most basic* skill of the trial lawyer.

The second basic skill of the trial lawyer is the proper, efficient, and orderly handling and introduction of tangible evidence. Again, however, a common criticism of the trial bar is its lack of facility in this truly simple undertaking.

This is all the more regrettable when one considers the highly persuasive quality of relevant exhibits. Jurors (and judges, too) trust them. They are the real thing. They do not exaggerate as witnesses do and they do not overstep their bounds as lawyers do. Many a case has been won or lost because a particularly intriguing exhibit was received in evidence or excluded.

The four touchstones for the handling and introduction of exhibits are:

1.   Authenticity
2.   Relevance
3.   The Hearsay Rule
4.   The Best Evidence Rule

These four touchstones must be satisfied before an exhibit can be received in evidence. Some call it "laying the foundation." By whatever phrase, the essential element is testimony establishing that the exhibit is authentic and relevant and complies with both the hearsay and best evidence rules.

Authenticity is simply a demonstration that the exhibit is what it purports to be. Is this thing — whatever it is — that is being offered in evidence, *prima facie* that which it purports to be?* The essential requirement is testimonial vouching for the thing unless, of course, authenticity is established by admissions in the pleadings, discovery, or a request to admit. See, for example, Federal Rule of Civil Procedure 36.

Relevance, as well as the hearsay and best evidence rules, is intrinsically dependent on the issues raised in the case and the purpose for which the exhibit is offered in evidence. In each instance, however, the foundation must be laid demonstrating that the exhibit is relevant and that it complies with the hearsay and best evidence rules.

---

*The standard is a *prima facie* showing of authenticity, as the court determines admissibility. Its weight is left to the fact-finder.

Potter v. Shrackle Problems

For each exhibit, counsel should check the four touchstones and then lay the foundation necessary for its admission in evidence through the testimony of one or more witnesses.

As in the case of witness examination, the skill of handling and introducing exhibits is developed by practice and is conducted with certain guidelines in mind.

1. Select with care the witness or witnesses you will use to lay the foundation for your exhibits. A mistake here could be fatal.

2. Because the introduction of exhibits usually is done through witnesses, keep in mind the basic principles of witness examination.

3. Have the exhibit marked for identification by the appropriate court official (usually the court reporter or clerk) at the earliest opportunity. Many lawyers have their exhibits marked for identification prior to trial in the sequence in which they expect to use them. Some judges insist on this. It is a good practice in cases involving many exhibits. But also consider the advantages to be gained from a brief pause (respite for the witness) and a little bit of the lawyer doing his or her "thing" that attends your stepping to the bench and requesting in a voice the jury can hear, "Your Honor, may the reporter mark this document (or object) defendant's exhibit 1 for identification?"

4. Once the exhibit has been marked for identification, include that identification in any reference you make to the exhibit and to it that your opponent, the witnesses, and the judge do likewise. Never permit the record to read merely, "this letter" or "that bottle" or "the photograph," etc.

5. Proceed to "lay the foundation" as follows:

    (a) Elicit from the authenticating witness those facts that qualify him or her to authenticate the exhibit. For example, have the witness say he saw the gun in the robber's hand.

    (b) Have the witness identify the exhibit by saying, for example, that State's Exhibit 1 is the gun (or looks like the gun) the witness saw in the robber's hand.

    (c) If the condition of the exhibit is a factor in its relevancy, either elicit testimony that its condition has not changed between the event and the time of trial, or offer a testimonial explanation of the change in condition.

    (d) If the exhibit is a reproduction of a place, a thing, or an event (e.g., a photograph or a tape recording), elicit testimony that it fairly and accurately portrays that which it purports to portray.

    (e) If more than one witness is required to authenticate or connect the exhibit, withhold your offer until you have completed your foundation. A premature offer and rejection can condition a judge to reject the exhibit later when the foundation has been completed.

6. Once the foundation for an exhibit has been laid properly, offer it in evidence and obtain a ruling on its admissibility. In some jurisdictions an exhibit may not be offered during cross examination, and in those instances the formal offer of the exhibit is reserved to your case in chief or rebuttal.

7. When you are opposing the introduction of an exhibit, you are entitled to conduct a cross examination on the foundation before the court rules on the offer. The scope of this cross examination, often referred to as a voir dire on the exhibit, is limited to the admissibility of the exhibit. The proponent of the exhibit should be alert to so limit the voir dire on the exhibit and not permit the opponent to conduct a general cross examination on the weight that is to be given to the exhibit.

8. When you are opposing the introduction of exhibits, be on the alert for changed conditions and distortions (particularly in photographs). Insist that an adequate testimonial explanation of the changes be given by the authenticating witness.

9. Do not permit your opponent to display tangible items in the presence of the jury until they are marked for identification and proffered to the witness for identification.

10. Keep a separate record of the status of your exhibits and those of your opponent. Know at all times their identification numbers, their general descriptions, the witness or witnesses who authenticated them, and whether they have been offered and received or excluded. Many lawyers keep a columnar record somewhat like this:

Plaintiff's Exhibits

No.	Description	Witness	Date or page of record offered	Date or page of record received	Date of page of record refused
1.	Letter from Jones	Smith	6/1/88 p. 138	6/1/88 p. 140	
2.	Hammer	Jones	6/2/88 p. 100		6/2/88 p. 210

11. At the close of your case, if you are uncertain as to the status of any of your exhibits, re-offer them before you rest.

Each exhibit has its own standards of authenticity and admissibility. For our purposes, they are better demonstrated than described.

PROBLEM 3

Photographs

In the *Potter v. Shrackle* case file, there are two photographs of Charles Shrackle's truck at the intersection of Kirby and Mattis. The photographs were taken by a police photographer approximately thirty minutes after the accident.

(a) For the plaintiff, introduce into evidence the photographs. You may use any witness(es) you desire (other than the defendant, Charles Shrackle) to lay the foundation for the exhibits. Examine the witness(es) to the extent necessary to lay the foundation and then offer the exhibits. Be prepared to discuss your choice of witness(es).

(b) For the defendants, oppose the examination of the witness(es) and the offer of the exhibits. Be prepared to voir dire the witness(es) on the admissibility of the exhibits.

PROBLEM 4

Photographs

In the *Potter v. Shrackle* case file, there are two photographs of Katherine Potter. The photograph of a smiling Katherine Potter was taken by her husband, Jeffrey Potter, at an outing approximately eighteen months before Katherine's death. The photograph of Katherine Potter lying on the pavement at the scene of the accident was taken by a newspaper photographer just before the ambulance attendants arrived.

(a) For the plaintiff, introduce into evidence the photographs. You may use any witness(es) you desire to lay the foundation for the exhibits. Examine the witness(es) to the extent necessary to lay the foundation and then offer the exhibits. Be prepared to discuss your choice of witness(es).

(b)   For the defendants, oppose the examination of the witness(es) and the offer of the exhibits. Be prepared to voir dire the witness(es) on the admissibility of the exhibits.

USE OF VISUAL AIDS

1. *Visual Aids in General.* In addition to exhibits that are offered and received in evidence on the basis of their intrinsic relevance to the case, visual aids frequently are used by lawyers during examinations of witnesses. These aids are exhibits that assist witnesses in explaining their testimony. Such exhibits, in and of themselves, are not relevant to the case; their relevance flows from the fact that by assisting a witness in testifying, they enhance the probative value of the testimony. The phrase "visual *aid*" as opposed to "demonstrative *evidence*" indicates that the exhibit's evidentiary value is derived from its role in assisting the witness as opposed to any intrinsic evidentiary value.

   The foundation for visual aids is based on the same four touchstones that govern other exhibits: authenticity, relevance, the hearsay rule, and the best evidence rule. For authenticity and the hearsay and best evidence rules, the foundation depends on the particular exhibit and will be determined on an individual basis. The general analysis of the necessary foundation, however, is the same as that used for all other exhibits.

   The relevance foundation for visual aids is testimony establishing that the exhibit will assist a witness in explaining his or her testimony. By permitting the court or the jury to more fully understand the value of the testimony of a witness, the exhibit enhances the probative value of the testimony. The countervailing arguments on the question of relevance are that the exhibit raises collateral issues, wastes time, or is unduly prejudicial. In ruling on the use of visual aids, courts employ the classic relevancy balancing test, meaning the use of such aids is discretionary with the court. Most judges are inclined to permit their use as aids to understanding witness testimony if they will not unduly emphasize that testimony.

2. *Diagrams.* In many jurisdictions, diagrams are *sui generis* and may be classified as either demonstrative evidence or visual aids depending on their relevance to the case. If testimony establishes that a diagram is a fair and accurate representation of something that is relevant, then the diagram is demonstrative evidence. The foundation required for diagrams is essentially the same as that required for photographs. (What is the purpose of the offer? Is the exhibit, when used for that purpose, relevant? Does the exhibit fairly and accurately represent what it purports to represent?) If what is depicted by an authentic diagram is not itself relevant to the case, the diagram is not admissible as demonstrative evidence. But if the diagram is authentic and will assist a witness in explaining his or her testimony, then it is helpful to a better understanding of the evidence and, thus, relevant. The diagram is then admissible as a visual aid for use in assisting the witness. In summary, a diagram usually is admissible as demonstrative evidence if it is authentic and in itself relevant to the case, and a diagram is admissible as a visual aid if it is authentic and will assist a witness in testifying.

   In some jurisdictions, however, diagrams are not admissible as demonstrative evidence under any circumstances and may be used in court solely as visual aids. Although a diagram may be authentic (i.e., it is what it purports to be), courts in those jurisdictions do not consider a diagram to be a sufficiently fair and accurate representation of the real thing to permit its admission as demonstrative evidence. Those courts' rationale is that a diagram by nature only depicts a one-dimensional view. Those courts do permit diagrams to be used to assist witnesses in testifying. In other words, they allow diagrams to be used as visual aids but not as demonstrative evidence.

In all jurisdictions, a diagram need not be drawn to scale to be admitted or used at trial. The fact that a diagram is not to scale affects its weight and not its admissibility or use. If the diagram is not being offered or represented as a scale drawing, then the fact-finder can consider and weigh that factor in evaluating the exhibit.

3. *Problems in the Use of Visual Aids.* Problems in the use of demonstrative or visual aids generally occur because of the lawyer's lack of skill in dealing with the device once he or she has been granted permission from the court to use it. One common shortcoming is the lawyer's failure to introduce the witness to the aid prior to the time he or she testifies. It is not sufficient that the witness be familiar with the subject matter illustrated in the aid. Unless the witness has n the device and has become sufficiently familiar with the particular illustration involved, the testimony can be disastrous.

The trial lawyers also should be careful to preserve the record for appeal. Words such as "right here" and "at this point" will not have meaning to an appellate court. If the witness' testimony is to have any value on appeal, it must be translated in some manner into words or markings.

PROBLEM 5

Chalkboard

Assume that the case is at trial and the plaintiff's first witness is Officer Michael Young.

(a) For the plaintiff, conduct a direct examination of Officer Young using the chalkboard as a demonstrative aid to illustrate his testimony.

(b) For the defendants, oppose the use of the chalkboard as a demonstrative aid and conduct a cross examination of Officer Young.

PROBLEM 6

Diagram

Assume that the case is at trial and the plaintiff's first witness is Officer Michael Young.

Prepare a diagram of the intersection of Kirby and Mattis that is large enough to be seen by a jury. the diagram in the case file, and add to or delete from it as you deem appropriate.

(a) For the plaintiff, conduct a direct examination of Officer Young, and either introduce the diagram as demonstrative evidence or use it as a demonstrative aid to illustrate his testimony.

(b) For the defendants, oppose the introduction or use of the diagram and conduct a cross examination of Officer Young.

IMPEACHMENT AND REHABILITATION OF WITNESSES

Impeachment

Although it is a part of the cross examiner's art, impeachment is a sufficiently difficult problem in itself to warrant separate consideration.

1. The cross examiner must consider not only how to impeach, but also whether the witness should be impeached at all. Just as the trial lawyer should not cross examine in some situations, he often may decide wisely that, although impeaching evidence is available, it should not be used. If the witness has not hurt your case, usually it is better not to impeach and risk offending the jury. If the testimony of a witness can be turned to your advantage, as in the case of a truly impartial expert witness, do so and do not impeach.

2. Foundation for impeachment by prior inconsistent statement:

    (a) Under the law of most jurisdictions, the witness must be confronted with a prior inconsistent statement during cross examination. If his or her attention has not been called to the earlier statement, extrinsic evidence of it will not be admissible. Cross examination should be specific as to the time, circumstances, and content of the earlier statement.

    (b) The rule requiring a foundation for prior inconsistent statements is relaxed under the Federal Rules of Evidence. Federal Rule 613(b) provides that the witness must be "afforded an opportunity to explain or deny" the prior inconsistent statement in order for extrinsic evidence to be admissible, but no time sequence is specified. Therefore, as long as the witness is available to explain the inconsistency if he so desires, extrinsic proof is admissible.

    (c) Most advocates will prefer to lay a foundation on cross examination regardless of whether or not it is required under the rules. The reason for this is twofold. First, the witness may admit the statement, making extrinsic evidence unnecessary. More significantly, confronting a witness with her own inconsistency often will have a dramatic impact that cannot be duplicated by introducing evidence of the earlier statement through another person.

3. If the witness denies making an earlier statement, be prepared to prove it by extrinsic evidence.

4. If the witness admits making an inconsistent or otherwise impeaching statement, do not ask questions that give him an opportunity to explain it away, unless you are certain that this cannot be done. The attorney who has called the witness will have an opportunity on redirect examination to elicit explanations, if any are available. This affords you the opportunity for recross.

5.   There is no need, and it is usually harmful, to dwell on the impeaching matter after it has been brought out in cross examination. Remember, you have a closing argument.

Rehabilitation

If a witness has been impeached during cross examination, counsel must evaluate whether to attempt to rehabilitate the witness on redirect examination.

1.   As with any redirect examination, counsel should limit the scope of the redirect to those items in which the witness needs an opportunity to explain or amplify upon his testimony after the cross examination. Redirect examination and rehabilitation of a witness is not the time to rehash the direct testimony once again.

2.   In considering whether to rehabilitate a witness on redirect examination, counsel should first of all be absolutely certain that the witness has, in fact, been impeached. If the witness has not been effectively impeached, do not attempt to rehabilitate the witness as you may only worsen matters.

3.   Rehabilitation generally consists of providing the witness with an opportunity to explain the circumstances pertaining to the impeachment and to elicit any "exculpatory" factors. Give the witness the opportunity to put the impeachment in context.

4.   If the impeachment can be explained, do it; if not, leave it alone on redirect as you just may worsen matters.

5.   If the witness has been impeached by a prior inconsistent statement, counsel should consider the admissibility of any prior consistent statements. 801(d)(1)(B) of the Federal Rules of Evidence. Prior consistent statements are generally admissible if they rebut an express or implied charge of recent fabrication.

PROBLEM 7

James Marshall

Part 1

Assume that James Marshall is called as a witness for the plaintiff and that he testified on direct examination that he saw Shrackle's truck hit the deceased as she was walking in the crosswalk.

Assume further that the statement contained in the case file does not exist. However, you (as the defendants' attorney) talked to Marshall a few days after the accident, and he told you that he had n Mrs. Potter walking on the sidewalk but had not n her either enter the crosswalk or get hit by the truck.

(a)   For the defendants, conduct a cross examination and impeachment of Mr. Marshall.

(b)   For the plaintiff, conduct any necessary redirect examination.

Part 2

Assume that Marshall testified on direct examination that he saw Shrackle's truck hit the deceased as she was walking in the crosswalk and that Marshall's statement exists as it appears in the case file.

(a)   For the defendants, conduct a cross examination and impeachment of Mr. Marshall.

(b)   For the plaintiff, conduct any necessary redirect examination.

ADVERSE EXAMINATION

Adverse examination is the examination of an opposing party or a witness that is specified as being adverse under the applicable evidence rules. Under the Federal Rules of Evidence, a witness who is "identified with the opposing party" is considered to be an adverse witness. See FRE 611(c) and the Advisory Committee's Notes.

In form, the party calling the witness, the adverse examiner, conducts a direct examination, and the opponent conducts a cross examination. In substance, however, the direct examination of the adverse witness involves the interrogation of an unwilling, biased, and unsympathetic witness, who has not been prepared by the party who has called the witness. The circumstances are the same as in cross examination and, therefore, leading questions are permitted.

After the adverse examination, the party opponent has an opportunity to cross examine the adverse witness. The form of the examination is that of cross examination, but that is typically not the substance of the interrogation. In other than multi-party cases, the witness is the cross examiner's client or a witness identified with the client. The witness has been prepared by the cross examiner and is certainly not unwilling, biased, or hostile. Essentially this is the same as a direct examination and leading questions usually will not be permitted. See FRE 611(c).

Different considerations may be involved in multi-party cases. It may be necessary to analyze each issue in the case to determine if there is adversity. Parties defendant may be adverse to each other on some issues and have a community of interest on others. Leading questions are appropriate only when there are adverse interests.

By calling an adverse witness, the examining party has the opportunity to determine the scope of the examination and thus to pick and choose what subjects are to be raised. Under the rules of most jurisdictions, including the federal rules, the cross examiner is limited to the scope of the adverse examination as determined by the examining party. Thus, the cross examination of an adverse witness is limited to the subjects brought out during the adverse examination.

Adverse examination, in the opinion of many trial lawyers, is the ultimate weapon. It is ultimate in the sense that it should be used rarely and then only with the greatest of care and control.

When it is employed, it usually is for a very limited purpose, e.g., to authenticate a document essential to the examiner's case. But there are occasions in which the trial lawyer will believe that tactics require a full, searching, in-court adverse examination.

Often lawyers will disagree on whether a particular situation is a proper setting for an adverse examination. There are at least two common bases for this disagreement. First, while the adverse examiner is not "bound" by the witness' testimony and may impeach the witness, the examiner nevertheless is eliciting the testimony during his or her case. Thus, if the adverse witness makes a good impression on the fact-finder, and his or her testimony is not helpful (or, worse, is harmful) to the examiner's case, the psychological effect on the fact-finder can be devastating to the examiner's case. The countervailing point is that the examining lawyer should be thoroughly prepared by depositions or investigation. The witness can and should be controlled by leading questions if there has been proper preparation.

Secondly, in many cases, selected portions of the adverse witness's deposition testimony are admissible on the offer of the examiner as admissions by a party opponent. This is a safer route to take and lawyers, being a cautious lot, frequently will opt for the safe route. The counterargument is that reading a deposition is a dry exercise, totally devoid of demeanor and not very persuasive. By using the deposition to control the live witness, however, counsel can make a point through the witness's own mouth, on the stand and under oath.

Despite these caveats about the use of the ultimate weapon, developing the skill of its use is mandatory. Here are some basic guidelines:

1. Frame your questions with great care. No "open" questions can be risked here. You may lead and you should do so.

2. Control the witness. Do not permit the witness to avoid the question. The witness must not be permitted to ramble or volunteer. Remember, you are entitled to responsive answers. Insist on them.

3. Never ask a question to which you do not know the answer and with which you cannot impeach the witness if he answers contrary to your expectation. Here, more than on cross examination, you will "get it" if you "ask for it."

4. Watch your attitude and demeanor toward the witness. Hostility toward any witness at any time is almost always counterproductive. Here, as on cross examination, there is a tendency to be hostile. You must guard against it. You have called the witness. If the fact-finder senses that you have done so for the purpose of humiliating the witness, it will be held against you.

5. When your adverse examination is concluded, be certain to limit your opponent's examination to those subjects you have covered. Do not permit your opponent to turn your effort into his or her own case.

PROBLEM 8

Charles Shrackle

Assume that the case is at trial and the plaintiff calls Charles Shrackle as an adverse witness.

(a)   For the plaintiff, conduct an adverse examination of Mr. Shrackle on whatever topics you think appropriate. Be ready to discuss: (1) any limitations you put on the scope of your examination; (2) the order of witnesses in which you called Mr. Shrackle; and (3) whether, in an actual trial, you would have called Mr. Shrackle.

(b)   For the defendants, conduct a cross examination of Mr. Shrackle.[**]

(c)   For the plaintiff, conduct any necessary re-adverse examination.

[**]*See* FRE 611(c) and the Advisory Committee's Notes.

DISCOVERY DEPOSITIONS

No factor has had a greater impact on the trial of lawsuits in the last forty years than the increased availability of discovery devices for learning about an opponent's case. In a civil case, if these devices are used properly, virtually nothing in your opponent's case should surprise you. Increasingly, this also is becoming true in criminal trials.

Following are a few words about what is perhaps the most important discovery device, the deposition:

1. In a deposition taken for purposes of discovery, the object is not to establish your own case or to impeach the witness. Rather, the goals are to obtain information for your use and to pin the witness down to a story for possible impeachment at trial.

2. Unlike cross examination, there usually is no need to cut the witness off if he gives a rambling answer. Let the witness tell his or her story; volunteered information may be useful.

3. Make sure, however, that the witness has stated his or her version of the events with sufficient certainty that the statements can be used for impeachment at trial. Once you are sure that the witness has made a firm and usable statement, leave the matter alone and go on to the next point.

4. Pursue all leads; do not avoid areas that are sensitive to your case. You will need to know what the witness will say, even though it hurts you.

5. If you are representing a deponent, or if the witness is friendly to your side of the case, ordinarily you should cross examine only when clarification of testimony might avoid or lessen the impact of some anticipated impeachment. Usually you will not cross examine at all.

6. Remember, however, that in most jurisdictions, a deposition may be read if the deponent is unavailable. Therefore, you should object to questions that are improper in form. You need not object to questions that ask for inadmissible evidence in order to prevent the use of that evidence at the trial.

7. If the question invades some area of privilege or violates another rule of evidence, and you do not want the witness to answer the question, you may advise your client that he need not respond. Counsel examining the witness should press for another answer until the witness has indicated that he or she will not answer. A court ruling on the propriety of the question can be obtained later.

PROBLEM 9

Alice Mallory

(a) For the plaintiff, take the discovery deposition of Alice Mallory.

(b) For the defendants, represent your clients' interests at the deposition.

[Mrs. Mallory will not be represented by counsel at the deposition.]

WITNESS PREPARATION

Chronologically, this topic should precede all that has gone before. As other teachers of trial advocacy have observed, however, exposure to the pitfalls of the courtroom sharpens the trial lawyer's awareness of the need for thorough witness preparation. (See, for example, the sequence of exercises in A. Levin and H. Cramer, *Trial Advocacy: Problems and Materials*, Foundation Press, 1968.) Hopefully, that has been the case here.

From a coaching standpoint, this topic might well be eliminated. In the privacy of a lawyer's office, there are no rules of evidence to restrain the preparation and examination of witnesses. Further, when one multiplies the lawyer types by the myriad of witness types, the number of combinations is infinite. Thus, it is impossible to actually teach witness preparation.

A great deal has been written on the subject. There are a variety of common sense admonitions calculated to put a witness in the most favorable and persuasive posture: be at ease; don't chew gum on the stand; dress neatly and conservatively; listen to the question and don't answer it until it is completed; don't worry about where counsel is going on direct or cross examination — just answer the questions.

There are, however, some questions about witness preparation and some problems which recur with remarkable frequency that should be raised. The following problems are intended to illustrate them. As you confront them, keep in mind that our English brothers at the bar seldom encounter them, for in England it is regarded as unethical for the barrister to "woodshed" the witness.

PROBLEM 10

Jeffrey Potter

The case is scheduled for trial in one week. Jeffrey Potter's lawyer, your partner, has just had a heart attack and will be unable to work for an indefinite period. He has asked you to take over the Potter case. You have met Jeffrey Potter but have never before discussed the case with him. However, he has agreed to have you handle the case. You need to discuss with him the trial in general and to prepare him to testify on the question of damages for loss of companionship and society.

Interview Jeffrey Potter and prepare him for trial.

ADVANCED DIRECT AND CROSS EXAMINATION

The Child Witness

PROBLEM 11

Vicki Williams

Assume that the plaintiff has presented his case, the defendants' motion for a directed verdict has been denied, and Charles Shrackle and Juanita Williams have testified for the defendants. The defendants' next witness is Vicki Williams, age 12. (Depending on the availability of a child witness, a witness of a younger age or different sex may be substituted.)

(a)   For the defendants, conduct a direct examination of Vicki Williams.

(b)   For the plaintiff, conduct a cross examination of Vicki Williams.

(c)   For the defendants, conduct any necessary redirect examination.

Proving Damages

Some of the most important and difficult issues in the examination of witnesses in civil cases concern damages. The following problems are intended to raise some of those issues.

PROBLEM 12

Jeffrey Potter

After introducing all available and admissible evidence on the question of liability, the plaintiff calls Jeffrey Potter. Assume that the jury will consider damages at the same time that it will consider liability. Assume further that the plaintiff intends to call both Professor Daniel Sloan and Professor Robert Glenn. Assume that the attached letter from Jeffrey Potter to Dr. Andrew Stevens of Stevens Counseling was produced during discovery. Plaintiff's claim of physician/patient privilege was rejected by the court. The letter is therefore available to counsel for use in the examination of Jeffrey Potter. The authenticity of the letter has been stipulated. Dr. Stevens is not available to any of the parties as a witness.

(b)   For the defendants, conduct a cross examination of Mr. Potter.

(c)   For the plaintiff, conduct any necessary redirect examination.

124 Bench Mark Lane
Nita City, Nita 99993
September 15, YR-4

Dr. Andrew Stevens
Stevens Counseling
1225 North Street
Lisle, Nita 99980

Dear Dr. Stevens:

I am sorry that payment for our last three sessions is late. I guess it goes without saying that Katherine and I don't see eye to eye on the need for this counseling, and it is very difficult for me to get her to even speak calmly about it, much less agree for us to pay for it. Nonetheless, I am enclosing our check in the amount of $300.

I am sorry that we can't continue with you. I thought your advice was very helpful and I appreciated the opportunity to talk with you about the problems that we have been having. I especially want to thank you for your concern about the issue of children. Of course, I agree with you that our primary responsibilities appear to be our careers, but my wanting to have children is becoming more important to me than perhaps Katherine's career.

Katherine and I have tried to have more discussions about the possibility of having children and the time it will take away from our respective careers. It is very difficult for her at this stage of her career to talk about children, but I know that she would really want to have children when she got to a stable position in her life. I know you understand how important this issue is to me, and that our marriage relationship depends upon our being able to get through this rather difficult period in our lives.

Your comments at the last session, that it was obvious to you that Katherine and I loved each other very much and would come out of this stronger than ever, make me smile and look forward to the future. I am sure that you are right. Perhaps when we have more time and her career isn't so hectic, I'll be able to persuade Katherine to come back with me to talk to you about the rest of our problems, which don't seem quite so important now.

Sincerely yours,

Jeffrey T. Potter

Jeffrey T. Potter

Potter v. Shrackle Problems

PROBLEM 13

Daniel Sloan

Assume that Jeffrey Potter has testified at the time indicated in the preceding problem. The plaintiff then calls Daniel Sloan.

(a)   For the plaintiff, conduct a direct examination of Professor Sloan.

(b)   For the defendants, conduct a cross examination of Professor Sloan.

(c)   For the plaintiff, conduct any necessary redirect examination.

PROBLEM 14

Jeffrey Potter

Repeat Problem 12. However, this time assume that Jeffrey Potter is highly emotional with regard to his wife's death.

(a)   For the plaintiff, conduct a direct examination of Mr. Potter.

(b)   For the defendants, conduct a cross examination of Mr. Potter.

(c)   For the plaintiff, conduct any necessary redirect examination.

PROBLEM 15

Jeffrey Potter

It has almost been a year and a half since Katherine's death. Jeffrey Potter is currently romantically involved with a young graduate student, Cheryl Tobias. He and Ms. Tobias met eight months ago and recently went to Martinique together. Jeffrey Potter is also aware of the economists' depositions.

As a witness, Mr. Potter may testify to any additional facts or events which are consistent with the facts set forth in the deposition. For example, he may testify, if plaintiff's attorney wishes to have him do so, about the specific sports or other interests which Jeffrey and Katherine Potter shared.

(a)   For the plaintiff, conduct the direct and redirect examination of Jeffrey Potter *as part of your case* on damages.

(b)   For the defendant, conduct the cross examination of Jeffrey Potter.

EXPERT WITNESSES

As a conservative estimate, eighty percent of all trials in courts of general jurisdiction involve the examination of skilled or expert witnesses. For example, in personal injury cases, there are medical experts and experts in accident reconstruction; in criminal cases, there are chemical, ballistics, fingerprint, and handwriting experts; and in commercial cases, there are economists and market analysts. The opportunities for use of skilled or expert witnesses are limited only by human knowledge and the trial lawyer's ingenuity. Accordingly, no lawyer is worthy of the name "trial lawyer" until she has mastered the techniques that attend the direct and cross examination of skilled or expert witnesses.

The function of the expert witness is to bring to the trial of a case knowledge beyond the everyday and to apply that knowledge to the facts in the case so that jurors may better determine the issues.

The basic guidelines are stated simply, but they are not so simple to apply.

1. *Qualifications.* The proposed expert witness must be qualified by training or experience in a recognized field of knowledge beyond that of the average layman.[***]

2. *Explanation of Expertise.* If the field of knowledge is at all esoteric, the expert witness should provide a brief explanation of it, particularly with reference to its application to the case at hand.

3. *Ruling on Qualifications as an Expert.* In some jurisdictions after the witness's qualifications have been elicited, the witness is tendered to the court as an expert in his or her field, and the court either accepts or rejects the witness as an expert at that time. Some courts, however, are reluctant to give their imprimatur to the witness' testimony or to rule on the witness's qualifications as an expert prior to hearing the actual opinion the expert will be asked to give. In those jurisdictions, the direct examination simply proceeds unless there is an objection, at which time the court rules.

4. *Cross Examination on Qualifications.* The opposing counsel may voir dire (cross examine) the witness on his or her qualifications at the time the witness is tendered to the court as an expert witness or, if that procedure is not utilized, before the witness is permitted to express her opinion.

[***]Under the Federal Rules of Evidence, the test is whether the witness' knowledge, training, or experience will *assist* the trier of fact in understanding the evidence or determining a fact in issue. Note also that the witness, if qualified as an expert, may testify in the form of an opinion *or otherwise.* FRE 702.

5. *Basis of Opinion.* The direct examination should elicit a description of what the expert did with regard to the case and the facts that are the basis of the opinion.[****]

The facts that may be used as the basis for the expert's opinion and may be elicited on direct examination are limited to those facts that:

(a)   The expert personally observed,

(b)   Were elicited in the courtroom and heard by the expert, or

(c)   Were transmitted to him hypothetically.

In the federal courts and in some state courts, facts that were made known to the expert outside of court, and other than by his or her own perception, may also be used if they are of a type reasonably relied upon by experts in the expert's field. FRE 703.

In most state courts, the hearsay rule and the other traditional principles of admissibility apply to expert testimony. Opposing counsel should keep an ear carefully tuned for the application of these principles during the expert's direct examination. In the federal courts and some state courts that have relaxed the hearsay rule and the other traditional requirements for admissibility for expert testimony, the expert may testify to, and base his opinion on, facts that are not admissible in evidence.

6. *Opinion.* The expert's opinion may not be speculation or conjecture. Rather, it must be an opinion to a reasonable degree of certainty within the expert's field. Most courts require that the opinion be elicited in a two-question sequence: (1) Do you have an opinion as to _____?, and then (2) What is that opinion? This gives opposing counsel an opportunity to object before the opinion is heard by the jury.

When the expert's opinion is based on facts that the expert did not personally observe or hear in the courtroom, the hypothetical question format is required in most state courts. However, in the federal courts and some state courts, the hypothetical question no longer is required, and

---

[****]In most state courts the direct examination *must* elicit the factual basis for the expert's opinion as a foundation prerequisite for the expert stating his opinion. This is the method for ensuring that the expert's opinion is based on admissible evidence.

While, in the federal courts, the underlying facts for the expert's opinion need not be disclosed on direct examination, the expert will be required to disclose them on cross examination. FRE 705. The court, however, has the discretion to require that the underlying facts be disclosed prior to the expert stating his opinion when the interest of justice so requires. *See* FRE 703.

The underlying facts for the expert's opinion are usually quite persuasive, and most trial lawyers will make them an integral part of their direct examination. The trial lawyer has the option in federal court, and she may tailor the direct examination to meet the needs of the particular case.

the trial lawyer has the option of using it or not. FRE 703, 705. When this format is optional, the trial lawyer's decision is a matter of trial strategy, which depends on many factors. Perhaps some of those factors will be demonstrated in the exercises.

The primary objections that are available to opposing counsel when the hypothetical question format is utilized are:

(a)   That the hypothetical question included facts not in evidence, or

(b)   That it did not include relevant facts that are in evidence.

Thus, in a complicated case the hypothetical question can be quite cumbersome. In anything but the most routine case, it can be a delicate procedure with pitfalls to snare the unwary.

7.   *Cross Examination.* The expert witness may be cross examined with respect to his or her opinion on the basis of:

(a)   The expert's qualifications,[*****]

(b)   Other facts in the case, or

(c)   The published opinions of other recognized authorities in the field (learned treatises).

[*****]The cross examination of qualifications, discussed in paragraph 4, is a *voir dire* on the admissibility of the expert's opinion. The cross examination here goes to the weight of the expert's opinion. Counsel should weigh carefully whether to cross examine in both instances or to elect one or the other.

Potter v. Shrackle Problems

PROBLEM 16

Robert Glenn

In the *Potter v. Shrackle* case, the plaintiff calls Professor Robert Glenn to testify on the issues of damages.

(a) For the plaintiff, conduct a direct examination of Professor Glenn.

(b) For the defendants, conduct a cross examination of Professor Glenn.

(c) For the plaintiff, conduct any necessary redirect examination.

JURY SELECTION

If one were to interview ten able trial lawyers at random with regard to how to select a jury, one would get ten different answers. The answers would range from, "Take the first twelve (or six) and put them in the box," to "Examine each juror firmly and searchingly." We will discuss the pros and cons of both attitudes as well as the way stations between.

There is virtual unanimity among trial lawyers that the makeup of the jury is important. There is also agreement among those who watch trial lawyers at work that we do a pretty fair job of jury selection, regardless of how we do it or why we excuse those who are excused.

There are certain basic guidelines that should be followed in selecting a jury:

1. In those jurisdictions that permit the lawyers to interrogate the veniremen, realize that this is your first direct contact with the jurors. Don't alienate them. Don't try them.

2. Know the statutory qualifications for jurors and the case law grounds for the challenge for cause.

3. Know the number of peremptories to which you are entitled.

4. Never challenge a juror for cause in the presence of that juror unless you have a peremptory by which you can excuse him if your challenge is overruled.

5. Use your peremptories wisely. Do not spend them too quickly.

6. Be alert for jurors whose background and experience indicate that they possess knowledge particularly relevant to the facts in the case. You may end up with a one-juror jury.

7. Be alert for jurors whose background and experience indicate a high potential of prejudgment of the case adverse to your position. They may hang the jury.

8. Seek a cross-section of the community, but bear in mind that studies have indicated a correlation between ethnic-socio-economic background and juror vote.

PROBLEM 17

Jury Selection in Potter v. Shrackle

Select a jury for one of the parties in the case. To permit an in-depth interrogation and analysis of each juror within a limited time frame, only four jurors will be selected. Each side will be limited to one peremptory challenge. Use the following jury information sheet.

Jury Information Sheet

Please assume the role of a person whom you know well, so you will be able to answer *voir dire* questions in that role. Please be realistic. Try to pick a role that will be commonly represented on jury panels *and not a role of an eccentric.* Your taking an eccentric role would seriously impair the realism and benefit of the exercise for your classmates, both those who serve as counsel and those who observe the exercise.

Please fill in the following form and be prepared to use it at the class session on Jury Selection. You may be asked to deliver it to the instructor in advance of the class or during the class session.

Your real name: _____

Information About You in Your Assumed Role

1. Name:_____
2. Age: _____
3. Address in Nita City: _____
    (Characterize the neighborhood:) _____
4. Length of residence in Nita City: _____
5. Occupation:_____
    Duties in that occupation: _____
6. Marital Status:_____
7. Number and ages of children: _____
8. Number of years of education: _____
9. Other relevant information:_____

OPENING STATEMENT

The opening statement is akin to the first scene in a play — it had better capture the audience. It is the trial lawyer's first direct contact with the jury, save in those jurisdictions that permit substantial lawyer participation in the voir dire examination of the jury. Even in those states, in the overwhelming majority of cases, it is the lawyer's first opportunity to present the jury with an intelligent, cohesive description of the case.

Some trial lawyers tend to minimize the importance of an opening statement. We do no. We regard it as crucial to the successful outcome of the trial.

There is no excuse for a poor opening statement (unless, of course, the case is so poor it should not be tried). The opening statement is essentially *ex parte*; it can and should be prepared well in advance of its presentation, and it should be rehearsed.

It is a skill that can be mastered with practice more readily than any other skill. The general guidelines for opening statements are:

1. Practice, rehearse, try out, and listen to your opening statements before you make them. You have a wife, a husband, a friend, a colleague who will listen if you ask. As you rehearse, you can listen, too. The preferred audience is a lay one.

2. Recognize the opening for what it is: a prologue or synopsis of a play, a blueprint, a travel guide folder, or the old favorite — the picture on the jigsaw puzzle box. We do not urge that you use these similes when you address the jury. We do urge that you recognize the opening statement for what it is. Indeed, in conjunction with the evidentiary portion of the trial and the closing argument, it is the trial lawyer's application of the oldest of public speaking techniques: tell your audience what you are going to say, say it, and tell them what you have said.

3. Recognize the opening statement for what it is not: it is not an argument. This is not the time to infer, plead, or fulminate. It is a time to tell the jury what the case is about and what you expect your evidence will be.

4. An opening statement in behalf of the plaintiff or prosecution should include:

    (a) A request of the court and the jury: "If the court please, ladies and gentlemen of the jury."

    (b) An introduction of yourself, your client, your opponent, and his client, if not already done sufficiently during jury selection.

    (c) A cohesive, succinct, and confident summary of what your evidence will be.

(d)   A conclusion, indicating that at the close of the case you will return and request the jury to find in favor of your client.

(e)   Some lawyers include the following either at the beginning or the end of the opening statement:

    (i)   A brief statement of the nature of the case.

    (ii)   A brief statement of the issues of the case.

    (iii)   A candid acknowledgment that the burden of persuasion rests on you and the degree of the burden.

    (iv)   A reading of the indictment or information (which is required in some jurisdictions).

5. An opening statement in behalf of the plaintiff or prosecution should *not* include:

(a)   Reference to evidence, or which the availability or admissibility is doubtful.

(b)   Anticipated defenses or defense evidence.

6. In most cases, an opening statement for a defendant should be made immediately following that of plaintiff or prosecution. If the court has granted you permission to defer your opening statement until the close of your opponent's case, be certain the jury knows this. Be very cautious about waiving a defendant's opening statement entirely.

7. An opening statement in behalf of a defendant should include:

(a)   A request of the court and the jury: "If the court please, ladies and gentlemen of the jury."

(b)   An introduction (or reintroduction) of yourself and your client, if not already done sufficiently during jury selection.

(c)   An admonition that opening statements are not evidence.

(d)   An acceptance of the issues as defined by your opponent, plus any additional ones that will be raised by the defense.

(e)   A reinforcement of the principle that the burden of persuasion rests with your opponent, plus a candid recognition of any issues in respect to which it rests with you.

(f)   A cohesive, succinct, and confident (but non-argumentative) reference to anticipated

Potter v. Shrackle Problems

deficiencies in your opponent's evidence, plus a like summary of what your evidence will be.

(g) A conclusion, indicating that at the close of the case you will return and request the jury to find in favor of your client.

8. As with your counterpart, a defense counsel's opening statement should not include references to evidence of which the availability or admissibility is doubtful.

9. Opening statements for defendant's in criminal cases often present special problems:

(a) Never assume the burden of proving innocence.

(b) If you have any doubt as to whether your client will testify, do not tell the jury he will. On the other hand, if you are certain he will testify, tell the jury and admonish it that it cannot fairly form any judgment in the case until it has heard from the defendant.

(c) We would not presume to outline an opening statement in a "no defense" criminal case. Perhaps we will one during our exercises.

10. In criminal cases, some jurisdictions permit counsel for the defendant to reserve opening statement until the close of the state's case-in-chief. Counsel should always consider very carefully the pros and cons of reserving the opening statement until after the state's case.

PROBLEM 18

Opening Statements in Potter v. Shrackle

Present an opening statement for one of the parties in the case.

CLOSING ARGUMENT

Here is the advocate in his final and finest hour! She won it with her closing argument! She was magnificent! Legion are the legends of summations.

A lawsuit is won during the trial, not at the conclusion of it. It is won by the witnesses and the exhibits and the manner in which the lawyer paces, spaces, and handles them.

The likelihood of a lawyer's snatching victory from the jaws of defeat with his or her closing argument is so slight that it hardly warrants consideration. (Compare last of the ninth multi-run, game-winning home runs; *but* Bobby Thompson's shot heard round the world in *Giants v. Dodgers* (1951).)

On the other hand, lawsuits are lost by fumbling, stumbling, incoherent, exaggerated, vindictive closing arguments.

This is not intended to minimize the importance of the closing argument. It is merely to relegate it to its proper position, which is a summation of the evidence that has preceded it, and a relation of that evidence to the issues in the case.

Although the closing argument is not quite as controllable as is the opening statement, it is very close to it — close enough that we can say that there is no excuse for a poor closing argument.

Many trial lawyers begin to prepare their closing arguments with their first contact with the case: as the facts make their initial impressions on their minds. That is when they are as close to being jurors as they ever will be. From that first impression forward they shape and reshape their closing arguments as the facts develop. Finally they shape the trial to what they believe their strongest arguments will be; they prove their arguments.

Thus, the closing argument has a considerable impact on the trial because an able trial lawyer knows that an argument without evidence to support it is no evidence at all.

The basic guidelines for closing arguments are:

1. Think about, prepare, and rehearse your closing argument before trial, leaving sufficient flexibility to meet the exigencies of trial.

2. Think about, modify, and rehearse your closing argument at each break in the trial in light of the record to date.

3. Think about, modify, and, if time permits, rehearse your closing argument at the close of the evidence and the conference on instructions.

4. Base your closing argument on the issues, the evidence, the burden of proof in the case, and your client's right to a verdict.

5. From the standpoint of format,

   (a) Address the court, the jury, and your opponent.

   (b) Tell the jury your purpose — to summarize the facts and relate them to the issues in the case.

   (c) Make your argument.

   (d) Tell the jury what its verdict should be.

   (e) Sit down.

6. From the standpoint of delivery: do not shout, do not engage in personalities, do not tell the jury what you believe, but act and speak as though you do believe, to the depths of your soul, every word you are uttering. If you can't do the latter, don't argue.

7. As for some of the canned approaches:

   (a) Do no repeat in chronological order the testimony of each witness. Give the jury some credit; it has heard the witnesses. Put it all together.

   (b) Do not tell the jury what you say is not evidence. Why belittle your argument? The judge will do that for you.

   (c) Do not assume a burden of persuasion that is not yours.

PROBLEM 19

Closing Arguments in Potter v. Shrackle

Present a closing argument for one of the parties in the case. In planning your closing, you may assume that you would have offered any or all of the admissible evidence available to your side at the trial.

Assume that all of the admissible evidence available to the other party has been offered. In many jurisdictions, counsel for the party with the burden of proof has the right to give the first closing argument and then a rebuttal argument to the defendant's closing. For the purposes of this problem, counsel for the party with the burden of proof should assume that their closing argument is the first closing argument.

SECTION II

CASE FILE

POTTER v. SHRACKLE and
THE SHRACKLE CONSTRUCTION CO.

TABLE OF CONTENTS

INTRODUCTION

This is a wrongful death action brought in the Nita state court by Jeffrey T. Potter, as administrator of the estate of his deceased wife, Katherine, and individually in his own behalf, against Charles T. Shrackle and The Shrackle Construction Company. Potter claims that Shrackle negligently drove the company's pickup truck, striking Katherine Potter as she was crossing the street, thus causing her death. Potter claims that Shrackle was acting in the course of the Shrackle Construction Company's business at the time of the accident.

Shrackle admits striking Mrs. Potter, but claims that she was crossing in the middle of the street, rather than in the pedestrian crosswalk, and that she did not look before entering the street in the path of Mr. Shrackle's pickup truck. Defendants deny that Shrackle was negligent and allege contributory negligence on the part of the deceased, Mrs. Potter.

The applicable law is contained statutes and the proposed jury instructions set forth at the end of the file.

All years in these materials are stated in the following form:

- YR-0 indicates the actual year in which the case is being tried (i.e., the present year);
- YR-1 indicates the next preceding year (please use the actual year);
- YR-2 indicates the second preceding year (please use the actual year,) etc.

SPECIAL INSTRUCTIONS FOR USE AS A FULL TRIAL

Issues for Trial

This case file may be used for a full trial on the issue of liability only or on the issues of both liability and damages. If used solely for the issue of liability, the proposed jury instructions should be modified accordingly by the deletion of instructions 15 and 16.

Witnesses

When this case file is used for a full trial, the following witnesses are available:

For the plaintiff:
  Officer Michael Young
  Marilyn Kelly
  Jim Marshall
  Jeffrey Potter
  Daniel Sloan
  Dr. Robert Glenn

For the defendants:
  Charles Shrackle
  Alice Mallory
  Victoria Williams
  Juanita Williams

A party need not call all of the persons listed as its witnesses. Any or all of the witnesses may be called by any party, subject to the limitations below. However, if a witness is to be called by a party other than the one for whom he or she is listed, the party for whom the witness is listed will select and prepare the witness.

Limitation on Witnesses

Each party is limited to four witnesses. To achieve this limitation for the plaintiff, Daniel Sloan's testimony is stipulated. (See the required stipulations below.) The plaintiff may call either Dr. Robert Glenn or Jim Marshall as a witness, and the testimony of the other witness is stipulated (see the required stipulations).

Required Stipulations

1. *Daniel Sloan.* The admissibility of the summary of his deposition is stipulated. Assume that Mr. Sloan is unavailable and his deposition is admissible under a state rule identical to Federal Rule of Civil Procedure 32(a)(3).

2. *Dr. Robert Glenn.* The admissibility of his report is stipulated. This stipulation is superseded if any party calls Dr. Glenn as a witness.

3. *Jim Marshall.* The admissibility of his statement is stipulated. This stipulation is superseded if any party calls Mr. Marshall as a witness.

IN THE CIRCUIT COURT OF
DARROW COUNTY, NITA
CIVIL DIVISION

Jeffrey T. Potter, the)
Administrator of the Estate)
of Katherine Potter, and)
Jeffrey T. Potter, individually,)
)
    Plaintiff,)
)
v.)   COMPLAINT
)
Charles T. Shrackle and)
The Shrackle Construction Company,)
)
    Defendants.)

Plaintiff for his Complaint against Defendants alleges:

FIRST CLAIM FOR RELIEF

1.   That at all times hereinafter mentioned, Plaintiff was, and still is, a resident of Darrow County, Nita.

2.   That at all times hereinafter mentioned, Defendant Charles T. Shrackle was, and still is, a resident of Darrow County, Nita, and the Defendant Shrackle Construction Company was, and still is, doing business in Darrow County, Nita.

3.   That Katherine Potter died on December 4, YR-2.

4.   That Plaintiff and the decedent Katherine Potter were married at the time of her death and had been married for eight years.

5.   That Plaintiff has been duly appointed the Administrator of Katherine Potter's estate.

6.   That on November 30, YR-2, at about 3:30 p.m., Katherine Potter was walking in an easterly direction across Mattis Avenue at the intersection of Mattis and Kirby Avenues in Nita City, Nita.

7.   At this time and place Defendant Charles T. Shrackle was driving a white YR-9 Chevrolet pickup truck which struck Katherine Potter, causing her serious injuries and that Katherine Potter died as a result of such injuries on December 4, YR-2.

8. That the pickup truck driven by Defendant Charles T. Shrackle was owned by the Defendant Shrackle Construction Company, and at the time Katherine Potter was struck by the truck, Charles T. Shrackle was performing duties for and acting on behalf of the Shrackle Construction Company.

9. That Defendant Charles T. Shrackle was driving the truck in a careless, negligent, and reckless manner, and in violation of his duties under Nita Revised Statutes 89-12 (4) (1968) to exercise due care to avoid striking the pedestrian Katherine Potter who was then lawfully walking across the street.

10. That Defendant Charles T. Shrackle carelessly, negligently, and in violation of Nita Revised Statutes 89-12 (4) (1968) failed to keep a proper lookout, to heed the fact that Katherine Potter was crossing the street in the immediate path of his truck, or to take any action to avoid striking Katherine Potter.

11. That Defendant Charles T. Shrackle carelessly, negligently, and in violation of Nita Revised Statutes 89-12 (4) (1968) failed to give proper warning of the sudden and unexpected approach of his truck either by sounding the horn or giving any other signal or warning.

12. That Defendant Charles T. Shrackle's negligence caused Katherine Potter to suffer severe physical and mental pain and suffering from the date such injuries were incurred on November 30, YR-2, until her death on December 4, YR-2.

13. That Defendant Charles T. Shrackle's negligence caused Katherine Potter to incur reasonable expenses for medical, hospital, and surgical care and the loss of wages from the time of the collision until her death, in the sum of $32,800.

14. That Defendant Charles T. Shrackle's negligence caused Jeffrey Potter, as personal representative of the Estate of Katherine Potter, to incur reasonable funeral and burial expenses, in the sum of $13,500.

SECOND CLAIM FOR RELIEF

15. Plaintiff re-alleges paragraphs 1 through 11.

16. That Defendant Charles T. Shrackle's negligence caused Jeffrey Potter, as the surviving spouse of Katherine Potter, to suffer damages for the loss of:

(a) The reasonably expected net income of Katherine Potter;

(b) Services, protection, care, and assistance of Katherine Potter, whether voluntary or obligatory, to Jeffrey Potter;

(c) Society, companionship, comfort, guidance, kindly offices, and advice of Katherine Potter to Jeffrey Potter.

WHEREFORE, Plaintiff demands judgment against Defendants, jointly and severally, in an amount in excess of $50,000, together with interest thereon and his costs herein, and for such other relief as the Court deems just and proper.

JURY DEMAND

Plaintiff demands a trial by jury in this action.

MADDEN & JAMES

by

William James

Attorneys for Plaintiff
Suite 720, Nita Bank Building
Nita City, Nita 99994
(721) 555-0003

DATED: April 7, YR-1

Return on Summons

I hereby certify that the above complaint was personally served on Charles T. Shrackle at his office at the Shrackle Construction Company, Nita City, Nita 99996.

Jane Bell

James Bell
Speedy Subpoena & Process, Inc.

Potter v. Shrackle Case File

IN THE CIRCUIT COURT OF
DARROW COUNTY, NITA
CIVIL DIVISION

Jeffrey T. Potter, the   )
Administrator of the Estate   )
of Katherine Potter, and   )
Jeffrey T. Potter, individually,   )
)
        Plaintiff,   )
)
v.   )   ANSWER
)
Charles T. Shrackle and   )
Shrackle Construction Company,   )
)
        Defendants.   )

Defendants for their Answer to Plaintiff's Complaint:

1.   Admit the allegations contained in paragraphs 1-5, 7.

2.   Admit that on November 30, YR-2, at or about 3:30 p.m.,
      Katherine Potter was crossing Mattis Avenue somewhere near
      the intersection of Kirby and Mattis Avenues. Defendants
      deny all other allegations in paragraph 6.

3.   Admit that the pickup truck driven by Charles T. Shrackle
      was owned by the Shrackle Construction Company. Defendants
      deny all other allegations in paragraph 8.

4.   Deny the allegations contained in paragraphs 9-14, 16.

FIRST AFFIRMATIVE DEFENSE

5.   Any injuries sustained or suffered by Katherine Potter at
      the time and place mentioned in the Complaint were caused,
      in whole or in part, or were contributed to, by the
      negligence of Katherine Potter and not by any negligence of
      Charles T. Shrackle.

SECOND AFFIRMATIVE DEFENSE

6.   Katherine Potter violated Nita Revised Statutes 89-12 (4)
      (1968) by failing to cross the street in the marked
      pedestrian crosswalk, to keep a proper lookout for vehicles
      using the roadway and to yield the right of way to any such
      vehicles.

WHEREFORE, Defendants demand that judgment be entered in favor of the Defendants with the costs and disbursements of this action.

PIERCE, JOHNSON & CLARK

by

James Barber

Attorneys for Defendants
Nita National Bank Plaza
Nita City, Nita 99994
(721) 555-6207

DATED: April 16, YR-1

Certificate of Service

I hereby certify that a copy of the above Answer was placed in the United States Mail, postage prepaid, addressed to the law firm of Madden & James, Suite 720, Nita Bank Building, Nita City, Nita 99994.

Marilyn Maxwell

Marilyn Maxwell
350 Court Place
Nita City, Nita 99993
(721) 555-4250

TRAFFIC ACCIDENT REPORT

N. C. Department of Motor Vehicles DMV-349 (Rev. 4-1-65)

DATE
Date of Accident: 11/30 19 YR-2   Day of Week: Friday   Hour: 3:28   A.M. ☐ P.M. ☒

LOCATION
Accident occurred: in Darrow   In City, County, or town of: Nita City
Outside City or Town ___ Miles ☐N ☐E ☐S ☐W of ___ (City or Town) Limits Center ☐ ☐
On: Mattis   Hwy. No. (I., U.S., N.C., R.P., R.U.)   at its intersection with ___ Street or Hwy. no.
If not at intersection, 52 ☐ Miles ☒ Feet ☐N ☐E ☒S ☐W From Kirby toward ___
If no Hwy. No. identify by name.   Highway No. or Adjacent County Line   Highway No., City, or Adjacent County Line

ACCIDENT TYPE

Ran off Road		Non-collision in Road			Collision of Motor Vehicle in Road With:						
1. Right	2. Left	3. Overturned	4. Other in road	5. Pedestrian	6. Other Motor Vehicle	7. Parked Vehicle	8. Train	9. Bicycle	10. Animal	11 Fixed Object	12. Other Object

No of Vehicles Involved: 1

VEHICLE NO. 1
Driver: Charles (First) T. (Middle) Shrackle (Last Name), 1701 W. Johnston (Street or RFD), Nita City (City and State)   Date of Birth: 8/13/YR-33 (Month, Date, Year)
Age 32 Sex M Race W Driving Experience 16 Years Driver's License: U311-5114-1161-146 ☒ Oper ☐ Chauff   NONE Specify Restriction   Member of Armed Forces: Yes ☐ No ☒
Veh: Year YR-9 Make Chevy Pick-up Color WHT Registration 232752B (Number) Nita (State) YR-2 (Year) M.V.No. ___
Amount of Damage: Owned By: Driver (Name)   Parts Damaged ___
Drivable: Yes ☐ No ☐ Vehicle Removed To Destination (Street or RFD)   By ___ (City and State)
$ NONE

VEHICLE NO. 2 OR PEDESTRIAN
Driver or Pedestrian: Katherine (First) (Middle) Potter (Last Name), 718 Flower Drive (Street or RFD), Nita City (City and State)   Date of Birth: 4/23/YR-30 (Month, Date, Year)
Age 28 Sex F Race W Driving Experience ___ Years Driver's License ___ (Number, State) ☐ Oper ☐ Chauff Specify Restriction   Member of Armed Forces: Yes ☐ No ☐
Veh: Year ___ Make ___ Color ___ Registration ___ (Number State Year) M.V.No. ___
Amount of Damage: Owned By: ___ (Name)   Parts Damaged ___
Drivable: Yes ☐ No ☐ Vehicle Removed To ___ (Street or RFD)   By ___ (City and State)
$ ___

Amt. of Dam. Other Property Damage ___   Owner and Address ___
$ ___

Injury Class
K. Killed   A. Visible sign of injury as bleeding wound, distorted member or had to be carried from scene   B. Other visible injury or bruises, abrasions, swelling, limping, etc.   C. No visible sign of injury but complaint of pain or momentary unconsciousness

INJURED PERSONS (Include fatally injured)

Veh.	Age	Sex	Race	Inj. Cl.	Name	Street or RFD	City	State
P	28	F	W	A	Katherine Potter (Died 12-4-YR-2 5:00 P.M.)	718 Flower Dr.	City	

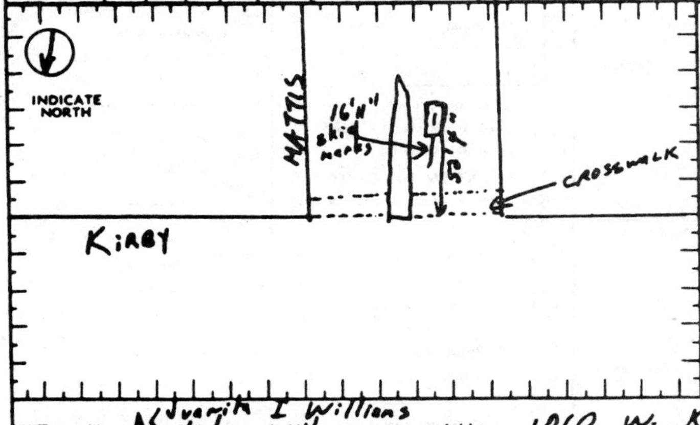

Injured taken to: City Hosp.

INDICATE NORTH (arrow pointing down/left)

Describe what happened: #1 was south bound on Mattis after turning left from Kirby He then struck pedestrian approx 30' south of pedes. crosswalk. #1 said he didn't see pedestrian until after he struck her. Witness A had been in car just in front of #1 and saw pedes. running across street westbound. Witness did not see actual contact. 12/3/YR1, witness B called station and said pedes was in crosswalk.

Tire impressions prior to impact: No. 1 16'11" No. 2 ___
Distance of travel after impact: No. 1 same No. 2 ___

Diagram labels: MATTIS, KIRBY, 16'11" skid marks, CROSSWALK

WITNESSES
Name A: Juanita I Williams / Vicky Williams Address: 1010 W. Kirby #15 City
Name B: Mrs. Dwight Kelly Address: 1910 Elden Lane - City
Name: ___ Address: ___

Arrests: Name ___ Charge(s) ___ (Cit. No.) ___
Name: ___ Charge(s) ___ (Cit. No.) ___

Sign Here: Michael Young (Officer's rank and name) 7319 (Number)   City (Department)   11/30/YR-2 (Date of report)

City Case No.	Authority for removal of vehicles:
	Veh. 1
Zone No.	Veh. 2
Tract No.	
If city vehicle or prop. dam. give name of liability ins. co.	Remarks:
Veh. 1	
Veh. 2	

VEHICLE 1   POINT OF INITIAL CONTACT

VEHICLE 2   POINT OF INITIAL CONTACT

DIRECTION OF TRAVEL
VEH. 1 ☐ ☐ ☒ ☐ ON _Mattis_
    N E S W

VEH. 2 ☐ ☐ ☐ ☐ ON _____
OR PED. N E S W

POLICE ACTIVITY

Time Notified of Accident   _11/30_ /YR2 3:28 ☐ a.m. ☒ p.m.
                              Date   Hour

Time Arrived at Scene   _11/30_ /YR2 3:31 ☐ a.m. ☒ p.m.
                                   Hour

Source of information: _____ (Officer at scene, drivers contacted station etc.)

ROADWAY FEATURE
(Check if applicable)
- ☐ 2. Bridge or Underpass
- ☐ 3. Driveway
- ☐ 4. Alley Intersection
- ☒ 5. Intersection of Two Roadways
- ☐ 6. Non-intersection Median Crossover
- ☐ 7. End or Beginning of Divided Highway

LOCALITY
(Check one)
- ☐ 8. Business
- ☒ 10. Residential
- ☐ 11. School & Playground
- ☐ 12. Open Country

FIXED OBJECT STRUCK
(Check first struck only)
- ☐ 1. Tree
- ☐ 2. Utility Pole
- ☐ 3. Fence or Fence Post
- ☐ 4. Guard Rail or Guard Post in Median
- ☐ 5. Guard Rail or Guard Post on Shoulder
- ☐ 6. Bridge
- ☐ 7. Underpass
- ☐ 8. Traffic island, curb, or median
- ☐ 9. Sign or Sign Post
- ☐ 10. Other Object
- ☐ 11. No object involved

ROAD CHARACTER
(Check one)
- ☒ 1. Straight road—level
- ☐ 2. Straight road—hillcrest
- ☐ 3. Straight road—on grade
- ☐ 4. Sharp Curve—level
- ☐ 5. Sharp curve—hillcrest
- ☐ 6. Sharp curve—on grade
- ☐ 7. Other curve—level
- ☐ 8. Other curve—hillcrest
- ☐ 9. Other curve—on grade

ROAD CONDITION
(Check one)
- ☐ 1. Dry
- ☐ 2. Wet
- ☐ 3. Oily
- ☐ 4. Muddy
- ☐ 5. Snowy
- ☐ 6. Icy

TRAFFIC CONTROL
(Check one or more)
- ☐ 1 Stop Sign
- ☐ 2 Yield Sign
- ☒ 3. Stop and Go Signal
- ☐ 4. Flashing Signal with Stop Sign
- ☐ 5. Flashing Signal without Stop Sign
- ☐ 6 R R Gate and Flasher
- ☐ 7. R. R. Flasher
- ☐ 8. Officer
- ☐ 9. Other Device
- ☐ 10 No Control Present
- ☐ 11. Control not operating properly
- ☐ 12 Control not visible or legible

ROAD DEFECTS
(Check one)
- ☐ 1. Loose material on surface
- ☐ 2 Holes, deep ruts
- ☐ 3 Low shoulders
- ☐ 4. Soft shoulders
- ☐ 5. Other defects
- ☐ 6 Road under construction
- ☒ 7 No defects

CONSTRUCTION
(Check one)
- ☒ 1. Concrete
- ☐ 2. Smooth Asphalt
- ☐ 3 Coarse Asphalt
- ☐ 4 Gravel
- ☐ 5. Dirt or Sand
- ☐ 6. Other _____ (Specify)

LIGHT CONDITION
(Check one)
- ☒ 1. Daylight
- ☐ 2. Dusk
- ☐ 3. Dawn
- ☐ 4. Darkness (street lighted)
- ☐ 5. Darkness (street not lighted)

WEATHER
(Check one)
- ☒ 1. Clear
- ☐ 2. Cloudy
- ☐ 3. Raining
- ☐ 4. Snowing
- ☐ 5. Fog
- ☐ 6. Sleet or Hail

VEHICLE TYPE

Vehicle 1 2
- ☐☐ 1 Car ☐ House Trailer ☐ Trailer
- ☐☐ 2 Taxicab
- ☒☐ 3. Truck—2 axles
- ☐☐ 4. Truck—3 axles
- ☐☐ 5 Truck-Tractor and Semi-Trailer
- ☐☐ 6. Truck and Trailer
- ☐☐ 7. Bus ..... (Specify)
- ☐☐ 8. Other _____ (Describe)
- ☐☐ 9 Emergency Vehicle

VEHICLE CONDITION
Vehicle 1 2 (Check one or more)
- ☐☐ 1 Defective brakes
- ☐☐ 2. Defective headlights
- ☐☐ 3. Defective rear lights
- ☐☐ 4. Defective steering
- ☐☐ 5. Defective tires
- ☐☐ 6 Other defective equipment (Specify)
- ☐☐ 7 Not known if defective
- ☒☐ 8 No defects detected

VISION OBSTRUCTION
(Check one)
Driver 1 2
- ☐☐ 10 Windshield or windows
- ☐☐ 11 Buildings, signs, bushes, etc.
- ☒☐ 12. No vision obstruction

Posted speed limit ...... mph
Speed of vehicle 1...... mph
Speed of vehicle 2...... mph

VIOLATION INDICATED
(Check one or more for each driver)
Driver 1 2
- ☐☐ 1. Exceeding stated limit
- ☐☐ 2 Failed to yield right of way
- ☐☐ 3 Drove left of center
- ☐☐ 4 Improper overtaking
- ☐☐ 5 Passed stop sign
- ☐☐ 6 Disregarded traffic signal
- ☐☐ 7 Followed too closely
- ☐☐ 8. Made improper turn
- ☐☐ 9. Improper or no signal
- ☐☐ 10 Improper parking location
- ☐☐ 11 Other improper driving _____ (Describe)
- ☒☐ 12 No violation indicated

WHAT DRIVERS WERE DOING BEFORE ACCIDENT
(NON-MOVING Vehicles)
Driver 1 2
- ☐☐ 10. Stopped in Travel Lane
- ☐☐ 11. Parked out of travel lanes
- ☐☐ 12. Parked in travel lanes
(MOVING Vehicles)
- ☒☐ 1. Going straight ahead
- ☐☐ 2. Changing Lanes or Merging
- ☐☐ 3. Passing
- ☐☐ 4. Making right turn
- ☐☐ 5 Making left turn
- ☐☐ 6 Making U turn
- ☐☐ 7. Backing
- ☐☐ 8. Slowing or Stopping
- ☐☐ 9. Starting in Roadway
- ☐☐ 10. Parking
- ☐☐ 11. Leaving Parked Position
- ☐☐ 12. All Other

WHAT PEDESTRIAN WAS DOING
(Check one)
- ☐ 1. Crossing at intersection
- ☒ 2 Crossing not at intersection
- ☐ 3. Coming from behind parked Vehicle
- ☐ 4. Walking in roadway with traffic
- ☐ 5 Walking in roadway against traffic
- ☐ 6 Getting on or off vehicle
- ☐ 7. Standing in roadway
- ☐ 8. Working in roadway
- ☐ 9. Playing in roadway
- ☐ 10. Lying in roadway
- ☐ 11 Other in roadway _____ (Specify)
- ☐ 12 Not in roadway

APPARENT PHYSICAL CONDITION
(Other than sobriety)
Driver 1 2 or PED.
- ☐☐ 1. Ill
- ☐☐ 2. Fatigued
- ☐☐ 3. Asleep
- ☐☐ 4 Other Physical Impairment
- ☐☐ 5 Restriction not Complied with
- ☒☐ 6. Normal
- ☐☒ 7 Condition not known

APPARENT SOBRIETY
- ☒☒ 10 Had not been drinking
- ☐☐ 11 Drinking—Ability impaired
- ☐☐ 12. Drinking—Unable to determine impairment
- ☐☐ 13. Chemical test given

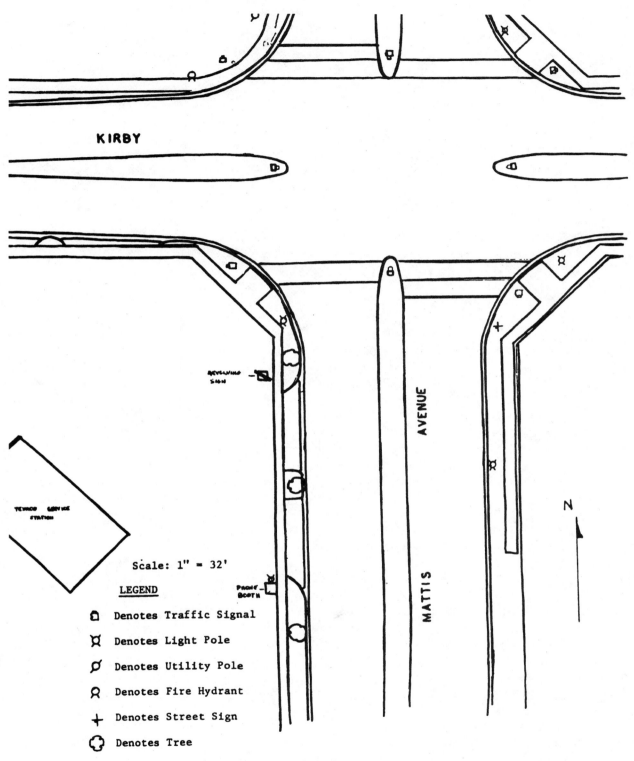

KIRBY

REVOLVING
SIGN

TEXACO SERVICE
STATION

AVENUE

MATTIS

N

Scale: 1" = 32'

LEGEND

⌂ Denotes Traffic Signal

¤ Denotes Light Pole

♂ Denotes Utility Pole

♀ Denotes Fire Hydrant

+ Denotes Street Sign

♣ Denotes Tree

PHONE
BOOTH

SCALE DRAWING OF INTERSECTION

Potter v. Shrackle Case File

Potter v. Shrackle Case File

Potter v. Shrackle Case File

Potter v. Shrackle Case File

Potter v. Shrackle Case File

–19–
Potter v. Shrackle Case File

–21–
Potter v. Shrackle Case File

Potter v. Shrackle Case File

STATEMENT OF MARILYN J. KELLY*

Re: Katherine Potter, deceased
Date of Accident: November 30, YR-2

My name is Marilyn J. Kelly. I live at 1910 Elder Lane, Nita City 99992. Telephone 555-1213.

On November 30, YR-2, at approximately 3:20 p.m., I was driving my car and was stopped in the easterly northbound lane on Mattis Avenue at the intersection of Mattis Avenue and Kirby Avenue in Nita City. The light had turned yellow as I approached the intersection, and I came to a complete stop with the front of my car just south of the crosswalk.

Just as I stopped, a small boy ran across the street from the west to east and barely avoided being struck by a car making a left turn from Kirby onto Mattis heading south. When he reached the sidewalk, I heard the crossing guard who was standing on the southeast corner of the intersection speak to the boy and say something to the effect that, "You have got to watch for cars."

I then saw a young woman with dark hair dressed in a white blouse, blue jacket, blue skirt, and beige shoes on the west side of Mattis Avenue. She was just stepping off the curb and starting to cross the street when I saw her. At that time the young woman was walking at a normal gait and was not running. She was definitely in the crosswalk, and I saw her take two or three steps.

I then glanced back up at the light, and at that time I heard a thud. I looked up and saw the young woman flying through the air and then land with arms outstretched on the front of the truck. She then went backward as if doing a backward somersault and fell under the truck. At that time I thought to myself, "My God, stop, don't run over her again." The truck driver appeared to be looking around immediately after the impact as though looking to see what he had hit.

The truck stopped at a point approximately fifty feet south of the south line of Kirby. At the point where the truck stopped the young woman was almost entirely underneath the truck. I definitely heard the thud before I heard the sound of any brakes shrieking. At the time of the thud the front of the truck was about even with the front of my car and was not completely straightened out from making the left turn.

---

*This statement was given to Officer Michael Young at the Nita City Police Department on December 4, YR-2.

The sun at the time of the occurrence was extremely bright and was coming from a southwesterly direction, and I had to shade my eyes when I looked back to the scene after the truck came to a stop.

After the truck stopped, a man ran out of the nearby gas station and the driver of the truck got out and went around to the front of the vehicle.

I do not know the Potter family, Mr. Shrackle, the driver of the truck, or anyone at Shrackle Construction Co.

I stayed at the scene for a couple of minutes, and then I left and went to my appointment at the beauty salon in the Lincolnshire Shopping Plaza.

The following morning at approximately 8:30, I read about the accident in the Nita City newspaper. The newspaper stated that the young woman was running and was approximately thirty feet south of the crosswalk at the time she was hit by the truck. I then telephoned the police and advised them that I had witnessed the accident, and that the young woman was in the crosswalk and that she was not running.

I have read the above and foregoing statement consisting of two pages and the same is true and correct.

Signed: *Marilyn J. Kelly*   Date: ___12/4/YR-2___
Marilyn J. Kelly

Witness: *Michael Young*   Date: ___12-4-YR-2___
Officer Michael Young
Nita City Police Department

Dec 12, Ye-2

Statement of James Marshall

I am the owner-operator of Jim Marshall's Texaco, 1601 Mattis, Nita City, Nita. I was working at the station on 11-30-Ye-2.

At approximately 3:30 on 11-30-Ye-2 I was looking out the ~~west~~ north bay of my station when I saw a dark-haired woman wearing a dress walking east on the south sidewalk of Kirby Ave. I looked at an employee to talk when I heard a thump. I looked out and saw a pickup truck carrying a body on the front of it. I sent an employee out to see if he could be of help while I called the police. I went out to see if I could be of help and saw the same woman that I'd seen earlier walking east on Kirby lying on the pavement.

Signed James Marshall

Witness: Joseph Lucey
Dec. 12, Ye-2

Editor's Note: Marshall's station is located on the southwest corner of Kirby and Mattis. This statement was taken by Joseph Lucey, an adjuster for the defendant's insurance carrier, at Marshall's station on December 12, YR-2, at about 11 A.M. The statement was written by Mr. Lucey. The signature and the correction are in Marshall's handwriting.

STATEMENT OF JUANITA WILLIAMS*

On November 30, YR-2, at approximately 3:30 p.m. at the corner of Kirby and Mattis, I was stopped on the west side of Kirby waiting for the light to change to green. A man in a white pickup truck was in the left-hand lane on the opposite side of Kirby with his left turn signal on as he was waiting to turn south on Mattis. The light changed to green, he waited until I had passed and with the light still green he turned south on Mattis.

I actually didn't see him hit the dark-haired woman, who I later found out was Mrs. Potter, but he could not have been going fast because I was only a few feet from the intersection when my daughter said, "Mother, I think someone has been hit." We immediately turned around and went back to the accident.

When we went back to the intersection, I saw the dark-haired woman lying underneath the white pickup truck. It was then that I learned the driver of the white pickup truck was Charles Shrackle of the Shrackle Construction Company and the dark-haired woman who was hit by the truck was Mrs. Potter.

I have read the above and it is my statement.

Signed _Juanita Williams_   Date: _____12/1/YR-2_____
Juanita Williams

Witness _Joseph Lucey_   Date: _____12/1/YR-2_____
Joseph Lucey

---

*This statement was given to Joseph Lucey, an adjuster for the defendant's insurance carrier, at Mrs. Williams' home on December 1, YR-2.

STATEMENT OF VICTORIA WILLIAMS*

As I was coming home from school on November 30, YR-2, about 3:30 p.m., we were headed east on Kirby Avenue. We were stopped at the intersection and a man in a white pickup truck was on the opposite side of Kirby in the left lane ready to make a left turn and go south on Mattis. We crossed the intersection, the man in the white truck waited for us to cross, and then he proceeded to turn the corner. A dark-haired woman was about twenty feet south of the crosswalk, on the median--facing my friends and with her back to me. She then stepped off the median into the path of the white truck. She was a little ways into the street when she was struck. I saw her purse fly in the air and I heard the screech of brakes.

I told my Mom that I thought someone had been hit, and we went back to the intersection. I saw the lady who was hit lying underneath the front of the white truck.

The police came and I found out that the driver of the white truck was Charles Shrackle and the woman was Mrs. Potter.

I am ten years old. My next birthday is next year.

I have read the above and it is my statement.

Signed _Victoria Williams_   Date: _____12/1/YR-2_____
Victoria Williams

Witness ___Joseph Lucey_____   Date: _____12/1/YR-2_____
Joseph Lucey

---

*This statement was given to Joseph Lucey, an adjuster for the defendant's insurance carrier, at Mrs. Williams' home on December 1, YR-2.

Potter v. Shrackle Case File

STATEMENT OF ALICE MALLORY*

My name is Alice Mallory. I am 47 years old. I am married and have two children, both of whom are in high school. I work part-time as a school crossing guard at the corner of Mattis and Kirby. I have done that work for about two years. I work both in the morning and in the afternoon at that corner.

On the afternoon of Nov. 30, YR-2, I was working on the southwest corner of the street. At about 3:25, I crossed over to the southeast corner of the street to reprimand a small boy who had not heeded my warning to stop. He had run out in front of some cars but wasn't hurt. As I knelt to talk to him, I saw over his head a young woman, who I later learned was Mrs. Katherine Potter, cross the street from west to east in the crosswalk. When she reached the median, she suddenly turned south and began to walk south on the median strip. I then looked down to continue talking to the boy. I then heard a thump and looked up instantly. I saw Mrs. Potter being carried on the hood of a pickup truck about thirty feet south of the crosswalk. The truck stopped about twenty feet later. I ran over to see if I could help, but others got there before me, so I returned to looking after the children.

At the time I was watching Mrs. Potter, I was also watching children on the other corner. However, I did see clearly all that I have said here. I did not come forward as a witness originally because I was upset and didn't want my story to hurt Mrs. Potter or her family. I was finally contacted by the defendant's lawyer and told her what I saw.

I have read the above and it is my statement.

Signed _____*Alice Mallory*_____   Date: _____June 7, YR-1_____
        Alice Mallory

Witness _____*Tracey Williams*_____   Date: _____June 7, YR-1_____
         Tracy Williams

_____

*This statement was given to Tracy Williams, an investigator for defense counsel, at Mallory's home on June 7, YR-1.

_____

In an answer to an interrogatory propounded by the plaintiff, the defendant listed the name of Alice Mallory as a person who had knowledge of relevant facts. The plaintiff's attorney has discovered that Mallory was a school crossing guard on duty at the intersection of Kirby and Mattis on the afternoon of the accident. In a conversation with the plaintiff's attorney, Mallory said only that she knows that Katherine Potter was out of the crosswalk at the time she was struck by Charles Shrackle's truck. Mallory refused to say anything more. The plaintiff's attorney received a copy of the above statement during discovery.

STATE OF NITA
DARROW COUNTY

IN THE MATTER OF   )

)

KATHERINE POTTER,   )   CORONER'S INQUEST

)

    Deceased.   )

A REPORT OF THE PROCEEDINGS

of a

CORONER'S INQUEST

over the body of

KATHERINE POTTER

Conducted by

Charles W. Wilson
Deputy Coroner
Darrow County

at

Darrow County Court House
Nita City, Nita

January 9, YR-1

DEPUTY CORONER:

Ladies and gentlemen, this is an inquest into the death of Katherine Potter, age 28, who was a graduate student at the University of Nita. Her home address was 718 Flower Drive in Nita City. She died at City Hospital on December 4, YR-2, at 5:00 p.m., from head injuries that she received as a result of being struck by a pickup truck, on November 30, YR-2, at about 3:28 p.m. on a city street in Nita City, Darrow County. As near as I can tell, it happened on Mattis Avenue near the intersection of Mattis and Kirby Avenues. We have one witness here tonight that we'll call on, the police officer who investigated this accident. Officer Michael Young, if you will come forward, please.

MICHAEL YOUNG was called as a witness herein by the deputy coroner, he was duly sworn and examined by the deputy coroner, and he testified as follows, to-wit:

Q: Would you state your name?

A: Michael Young.

Q: And your occupation?

A: Police officer for the Nita City Police Department.

Q: On Nov. 30, YR-2, did you investigate an accident on Mattis Avenue just south of Kirby?

A: Yes, sir, I did.

Q: What was the weather that day, was it clear, or--

A: Yes, it was clear.

Q: Pavement dry?

A: The pavement was dry. The sun was shining.

Q: And is that a four-lane road where this happened? In other words, could two cars be going south and two north at that particular spot?

A: Yes, sir, four-lane, two lanes each way.

Q: With a median in between them?

A: Yes, a concrete median.

Q: Now, how wide is that median, do you have any idea?

A: I would estimate it to be about four to five feet.

Q: What direction was Katherine Potter traveling, from east to west or west to east?

A: I have conflicting reports on that. I have two people who state that she was eastbound and one who says she was westbound.

Q: This pickup truck that was involved in this, what was the name of the man who owned and drove it?

A: Charles T. Shrackle was driving, and the truck was owned by The Shrackle Construction Co.

Q: And what--was he going straight ahead or had he just made a turn off of Kirby?

A: He was making a left turn from Kirby onto Mattis, South Mattis.

Q: And could he have been traveling at any excessive rate of speed?

A: I don't believe so.

Q: In that distance it would be pretty hard, I believe, the distance that was traveled.

A: Yes, sir.

Q: Now, did he say whether he saw this lady or not?

A: No sir, he did not see her at all.

Q: There are stop lights at that particular intersection?

A: Yes, sir.

Q: Did he have the green light or did he stop on the--did he have the stop light and then start from a stop?

A: He had the green light, had to wait for one car to pass before he made his turn.

Q: Do you know what color clothing she was wearing?

A: I believe she had on a blue skirt with a blue jacket and a white blouse.

Q: Was she still at the scene when you arrived?

A: Yes, sir.

Q: And how far away were you when you received your call to go to the scene?

A: I was in the 900 block of West Springfield Street when they directed me to the accident scene.

Q: You were not too far away, then?

A: No, sir.

Q: And she was taken by ambulance to City Hospital at that time?

A: Yes, sir.

Q: Now, the driver of the pickup truck had a valid driver's license, I presume?

A: Yes, sir.

Q: And there were no restrictions?

A: No, sir.

Q: And there was no one else hurt in this accident?

A: No, sir.

Q: Was there any evidence of any alcoholic beverages being consumed by either party?

A: No, sir.

Q: And there was just the party in the truck, the driver of the truck?

A: Yes, sir.

Q: And what is his occupation, do you happen to know that?

A: I believe he's a contractor.

Q: Did he have work, south of where this happened, going on at the time--or do you know that?

A: I don't know where he was headed for, sir.

Q: Did the pedestrian cross at the pedestrian crosswalk?

A: I have one witness who says that she didn't, and I have two other witnesses who say that she did.

Q: Is there any evidence--was there any evidence as to where she was--the point of impact, did you ever find out approximately where in the street that was?

A: I was unable to determine that. I looked for broken glass and other items, but there were none.

Q: Would she have had any occasion to have been south of that intersection? Do you know where she had been or where she was going?

A: I don't know, no. She lived west of that intersection and I have no idea what her travels were.

Q: Did she have any children in school?

A: I don't believe she had any children at all.

Q: There is a school on up there as I understand.

A: Yes, sir.

Q: Elementary school. Do you have anything further you would like to add?

A: To clear up the witnesses on the accident. At the time I made out the report that you are reading from right there, I only had two, and one of them placed Mrs. Potter out of the crosswalk and south of the intersection. However, the next day, when the newspaper account came out about the accident, I had another lady call in and state that she saw it and this was wrong. And I've taken statements from her and the other witnesses there, plus the fact that a gas station attendant saw her shortly before the accident. We took a statement from him, also.

A: And he said that she was in the crosswalk?

A: Yes, sir.

Q: And what is the name of the gas station attendant and his address, do you have that?

A: That's Jim Marshall's Texaco Station, at 1601 South Mattis.

Q: And this was Jim Marshall, himself, that gave you this statement?

A: Yes, sir.

Q: And the other statement was given by whom?

A: A Marilyn J. Kelly. She lives at 1910 Elder Lane, that's
     E-l-d-e-r, in Nita City.

Q: Were either one of these people acquainted with Mrs. Potter?

A: As far as I know, no, sir.

Q: Now, the person that gave you the statement that she was not
     in the crosswalk, what was--what was that name?

A: That was Mrs. Kelly.

Q: And where does she live and where was she--

A: I beg your pardon, my mistake, I have to find my other
     statement. That was a Victoria Williams.

Q: Where was she when this accident happened, do you know that?
A: She was in a car that was driven by her mother, Mrs. Juanita
     Williams, that was eastbound on Kirby at the time of the
     accident.

Q: And was she west of the stop light or east of the stoplight?
A: At the time of the accident she would have to be east of the
     stop light, because it was--

Q: She would have been looking back, then?

A: Yes, sir.

Q: Isn't that a little strange for a person to be looking
     back--what age was that person?

A: Ten years old.

Q: That was the only person that put her outside the crosswalk,
     right?

A: Yes, sir.

Q: The other two people are of age?

A: Yes, sir.

Q: And the person in Jim Marshall's gas station would be
     looking almost directly across the intersection--

A: That is correct.

Q: (Continuing)--from the gas station. Where was he in the gas station area, do you know?

A: He was at the western--or northwest bay area of the gas station at the time that he saw Mrs. Potter.

Q: That would put him almost in a direct line with the crosswalk?

A: Approximately.

Q: (continuing)--more so than in the south bay, as I understand that gas station.

A: That's correct sir.

Q: Now, the other person, where was she?

A: She was at the stop light facing north on Mattis at Kirby waiting for the light to change so she could go on through the intersection.

Q: In other words, she was south of Mrs. Potter when she would go across the crosswalk, is that correct?

A: That is correct.

Q: In other words, this first report that was written could conceivably be wrong?

A: That's correct, sir.

Q: That she probably was in the crosswalk, to the best of your knowledge at the present time?

A: I believe so.

Q: From the witnesses you have talked to since that time?

A: Yes, sir.

Q: Now, have you talked to any other witnesses that saw this?

A: No, sir, these are the only ones.

Q: Is there any obstruction in that particular intersection that could cause a driver not to see a person?

A: No, sir.

Q: What year pickup truck was this that struck Mrs. Potter?

A: I believe it was a YR-9 Chevrolet Camaro--not Camaro--what do you call them?

Q: A Chevy, anyway.

A: Right.

Q: Would that have--did you observe whether the windshield was clean or dirty and is the visibility as good on a YR-9 as it would be on a later model, we'll say?

A: I believe the visibility is as good as on a later model and the windshield was clean.

Q: Do any of the jurors have any questions they'd like to ask Officer Young at this time? Do you have anything further you would like to add?

A: No, sir.

Q: On behalf of the People of this County and the State of Nita, I'd like to thank you for doing a fine job of investigation. You're excused.

(Witness excused)

CORONER: Members of the jury, that concludes the witnesses that we have in this particular death. I might remind you that you can arrive at any one of these verdicts--(1) death by accident, (2) death by suicide, or (3) death by homicide. If you will retire out this door and to your right into the library, and then deliberate and render to me as coroner of this county a verdict, I will certainly appreciate it.

(Thereupon, the jury retired, and thereafter returned, and the following proceedings were had):

CORONER: Members of the jury, have you reached a verdict?

FOREMAN: Yes.

CORONER: And what is that verdict, Mr. Foreman, just the part you have written?

FOREMAN: Death by accident.

CORONER: And this is signed by all the jurors?

FOREMAN: All the jurors.

CORONER: Thank you. That concludes this inquest.

I hereby certify that this is a true and correct transcription of the proceedings and verdict of the Inquest into the death of

Katherine Potter conducted on January 9, YR-1, at the Darrow County Courthouse, Nita City, Nita.

Certified by:

Matilda Smith
Matilda Smith
Court Reporter

DEPOSITION OF CHARLES T. SHRACKLE

CHARLES T. SHRACKLE, the defendant, called to testify on
deposition by the plaintiff and having been duly sworn, testified
as follows:

EXAMINATION BY MR. JAMES (counsel for plaintiff):

Q: Would you please state your name, age, and address?

A: Charles T. Shrackle, 1701 West Johnston, Nita City, 32 years
      old.

Q: What is your business or occupation?

A: I'm a self-employed excavating contractor.

Q: And, is your contracting business limited solely to
      excavation?

A: Yes.

Q: All right. And, how long have you been so self-employed?

A: Since YR-4 . . . September of YR-4.

Q: All right. And, what is the name of your company?

A: Shrackle Construction Company.

Q: Is that a corporation?

A: Yes, it is.

Q: Who are the stockholders?

A: My wife and I. It's a small business corporation.

Q: What time did you arise on the morning of November 30, YR-2?

A: Six forty-five a.m.

Q: Is that your usual and customary time of arising?

A: Yes.

Q: Approximately how many hours of sleep had you had the night
      before?

```
 1
 2   A:   Seven.
 3
 4   Q:   Were you taking any medication or drugs at that time?
 5
 6   A:   No.
 7
 8   Q:   How was the state of your health on that date?
 9
10   A:   Fine.
11
12   Q:   Would you briefly describe for us what you did that day
13        prior to three o'clock p.m.?
14
15   A:   I went to my office.
16
17   Q:   Where is that located?
18
19   A:   On Route 45 in Sommers Township, and started my crews
20        working and then went to the corner of John and Holiday Park
21        and worked on--at that--at that job for the remainder of the
22        day.
23
24   Q:   All right. And what was that job?
25
26   A:   We were installing a sewer and putting the finishing touches
27        on a sewer we had installed there.
28
29   Q:   All right. And, how long did you stay at that job?
30
31   A:   Until approximately 2:30 p.m.
32
33   Q:   All right. Then, where did you go?
34
35   A:   To Nita Builders Supply.
36
37   Q:   Where is that located?
38
39   A:   At 30 East John, Nita City.
40
41   Q:   What, then, did you do?
42
43   A:   Ordered some material, talked to the--some of the people in
44        the office there and one of my men came in. I talked to him
45        for a few minutes and then proceeded to Greenbriar Manor.
46
47   Q:   All right. Now, you, at the time of this occurrence, you
48        were going to Greenbriar Manor?
49
50   A:   That's right.
51
52   Q:   That is located on South Mattis Avenue?
```

```
 1    A:   That's right.
 2
 3    Q:   How did you proceed from 30 East John Street to the inter
 4         section of Kirby and Mattis?
 5
 6    A:   As I recall, I left Builders Supply and went to First Street
 7         and turned south to Kirby, and proceeded straight across
 8         Kirby.
 9
10    Q:   Okay. And approximately what time did you leave Builders
11         Supply?
12
13    A:   That would be difficult for me to say. I would say around
14         three o'clock p.m. I don't--can't say.
15
16    Q:   And, about what time did you arrive at the intersection of
17         Mattis and Kirby?
18
19    A:   That I do not know for sure.
20
21    Q:   Did you go directly?
22
23    A:   Yes.
24
25    Q:   Did you have a job in progress at Greenbriar Manor?
26
27    A:   Yes.
28
29    Q:   What was the nature of that work?
30
31    A:   We were doing some excavating work for sewer lines that were
32         to be laid for an addition they're putting on.
33
34    Q:   Was anyone with you at that time?
35
36    A:   No.
37
38    Q:   As you got to the intersection of Mattis and Kirby, do you
39         recall whether the traffic light was red or green in your
40         favor?
41
42    A:   Green, in my favor.
43
44    Q:   And, what were the traffic conditions at that time?
45
46    A:   I would say moderate traffic. The intersection was busy.
47
48    Q:   Did you come to a complete stop at any time after you
49         entered the intersection itself?
50
51    A:   No.
52
```

```
 1    Q:   Did you have to wait for any traffic to clear before you
 2         made your left turn?
 3
 4    A:   I slowed for a vehicle that went by.
 5
 6    Q:   Now, you were proceeding west on Kirby Avenue and were
 7         turning south onto Mattis?
 8
 9    A:   Yes.
10
11    Q:   And you would have been turning left?
12
13    A:   Yes.
14
15    Q:   From where did you start your left turn?
16
17    A:   I'm sorry, I don't understand.
18
19    Q:   Were you in the southernmost, westbound lane of Kirby at the
20         time you started your turn?
21
22    A:   Yes, I was, yes.
23
24    Q:   And, did you make a gradual turn or sharp turn?
25
26    A:   I made what I would consider a gradual turn to the east lane
27         of Mattis--southbound on Mattis.
28
29    Q:   And, did you have to wait for any vehicles to go through the
30         intersection before you could complete your turn?
31
32    A:   No.
33
34    Q:   I believe you testified that you waited for one car to pass?
35
36    A:   That--to complete my turn, you mean? I waited for one car to
37         go through the intersection as I was approaching the
38         intersection. That car passed through the intersection as I
39         was approaching--I slowed down for it to pass through, I
40         didn't have to come to a complete stop, just slowed down.
41
42    Q:   All right. There was just the one car?
43
44    A:   Yes.
45
46    Q:   Okay. Did you observe any school children at or near the
47         intersection?
48
49    A:   Yes.
50
51    Q:   And about how many children did you observe?
52
```

```
 1    A:    I believe three.
 2
 3    Q:    All right. Where were they located?
 4
 5    A:    They were on the corner of--it would have been the south--it          ✱
 6          would have been the southwest corner of the intersection--
 7          where the Texaco station is.
 8
 9    Q:    All right. They would have been on the southwest corner,
10          then, next to the Texaco station?
11
12    A:    Yes.
13
14    Q:    All right. And, were they standing or were they walking?                ✱
15
16    A:    Standing.
17
18    Q:    All right. Do you know what direction they were facing?
19
20    A:    No.
21
22    Q:    Did you observe a school crossing guard at that time?                   ✱
23
24    A:    Yes.
25
26    Q:    Where was she located?
27
28    A:    She was standing on the other corner.
29
30    Q:    On the southeast corner?
31
32    A:    Yes.
33
34    Q:    Did you see any other pedestrians at that time?
35
36    A:    No sir.
37
38    Q:    Do you know what color clothes the children had on?
39
40    A:    No.
41
42    Q:    Do you know the names of the children that you saw?
43
44    A:    No.
45
46    Q:    Mr. Shrackle, would you describe for us, please, what
47          happened from the time you approached the intersection until
48          the actual impact occurred?
49
50    A:    Well, I approached the intersection and made the turn, and     ✱
51          there was--there were cars coming from the west and I made
52          the turn and there--and the impact and that was it.
```

```
 1    Q:    Do you know approximately where the impact--the first impact
 2          occurred?
 3
 4    MR. BARBER (counsel for defendants): With relation to what?
 5
 6    THE WITNESS:  Yes.
 7
 8    MR. JAMES (counsel for plaintiff): With relation to the south
 9    curb line of Kirby Avenue.
10
11    A:    I would say that--no, I don't know.
12
13  ⋫ Q:    Did you see Mrs. Potter at any time prior to the impact?
14
15    A:    No, sir.
16
17  ⋫ Q:    Did you apply your brakes at any time prior to the impact?
18
19    A:    No, sir.
20
21  ⋎ Q:    What was the condition of your automobile at that time?
22
23    A:    Fine.
24
25    Q:    What type of a vehicle were you driving?
26
27    A:    YR-9 El Camino.
28
29    Q:    And what type of license tags did you have on the truck?
30
31    A:    Standard pickup truck type.
32
33    Q:    And those are subject to inspection by the state of Nita?
34
35    A:    Yes, they are.
36
37    Q:    What is the date of the last inspection prior to
38          November 30, YR-2?
39
40    A:    I would have to check my records to find out.
41
42    Q:    What was the condition of the tires on your vehicle at that
43          time?
44
45    A:    They were new--relatively new. They were purchased--I could
46          check the date for you, but they were purchased not very
47          long before. They had, I think, less than five thousand
48          miles on them.
49
50    Q:    And, had you had the brakes worked on at any time within the
51          preceding six months?
52
```

Handwritten near line 27:
$$\frac{1947}{1988}$$ (with "8" above "7" and "9" above)

```
 1   A:   Adjusted by myself, but that's all.
 2
 3   Q:   And, would you characterize them as being in good working
 4        order?
 5
 6   A:   Yes.
 7
 8   Q:   What was the condition of the pavement?
 9
10   A:   Dry.
11
12   Q:   And, the weather conditions?
13
14   A:   Clear.
15
16   Q:   Was the sun shining?
17
18   A:   Yes.
19
20   Q:   What did you do after--immediately after the impact, when
21        you were first aware that your vehicle stopped something--
22        struck something?
23
24   A:   Stopped--applied the brakes.
25
26   Q:   Were you able to observe anything at that time as to whether
27        Mrs. Potter went immediately under your truck or was thrown
28        up in the air?
29
30   A:   No, sir, I wasn't.
31
32   Q:   Do you know approximately how far from the south curb line
33        of Kirby that your vehicle came to a rest?
34
35   A:   No, sir, but the officer has that measurement.
36
37   Q:   Do you know your approximate speed as you were in the
38        process of making your turn?
39
40   A:   No, I don't. I would say around fifteen miles an hour.
41
42   Q:   As you were making your turn, did you observe any
43        automobiles stopped on Mattis waiting for the light to turn?
44
45   MR. BARBER (counsel for defendants): Where?
46
47   MR. JAMES(counsel for plaintiff): Either southbound or
48        northbound.
49
50   THE WITNESS: Would you repeat that? I'm sorry.
51
52
```

```
 1   MR. JAMES (counsel for plaintiff): As you were making your turn,
 2       did you observe any vehicles stopped on Mattis waiting for
 3       the light to turn in their favor?
 4
 5   A:  Yes, I believe there were vehicles in the southbound lane of
 6       Mattis, waiting to turn, yes.
 7
 8   Q:  All right. Did you observe any vehicles in the northbound
 9       lane of Mattis?
10
11   A:  No, I did not.
12
13   Q:  Had you consumed any alcoholic beverages on the date of
14       November 30, YR-2?
15
16   A:  No, sir.
17
18   Q:  On that date were you covered by a liability insurance
19       policy?
20
21   A:  Yes.
22
23   Q:  And what company was that with?
24
25   A:  Boston Casualty.
26
27   Q:  Do you know what the policy coverage was--the limits of
28       insurance afforded by that policy?
29
30   A:  I believe Mr. Barber would know that.
31
32   MR. BARBER (counsel for defendants): Go ahead. I'll find it for
33       you.
34
35       Under policy FA 606560 and effective September 23, YR-2 to
36       September 23, YR-1, automobile liability coverage of
37       $200,000 per person, and $500,000 per accident. They have
38       sent a letter to Mr. Shrackle advising him that the ad
39       damnum is in excess of the policy limits.
40
41   MR. JAMES (counsel for plaintiff): As best you know, have you
42       complied with all the conditions of the policy--
43
44   A:  Yes.
45
46   Q:  (Continuing)--required?
47
48   MR. BARBER (counsel for defendants): I have been advised of no
49       policy defenses or--
50
51
52
```

1   MR. JAMES (counsel for plaintiff): The company has never
2   indicated to you--
3
4   MR. BARBER (counsel for defendants): Boston has never indicated
5   anything of that nature.
6
7   MR. JAMES (counsel for plaintiff): Did you have any other
8   insurance, either a general contractor's liability policy or
9   an umbrella type of coverage--
10
11   A: No, sir.
12
13   Q: (Continuing)--that would have--okay. Are you the named
14   insured on that policy?
15
16   A: Yes, doing business--
17
18   Q: As Shrackle Construction Company?
19
20   A: Yes.
21
22   Q: Did you file personal income tax returns for the years YR-5
23   through YR-3?
24
25   A: Yes.
26
27   Q: And, did you file those either in Nita City at the proper
28   time or in Memphis, Tennessee, at the proper time?
29
30   A: Yes.
31
32   Q: What was your approximate adjusted gross income?
33
34   MR. BARBER (counsel for defendants): You don't need to answer
35   that. You can wrestle with me for that over at the
36   courthouse.
37
38   MR. JAMES (counsel for plaintiff): I have no further questions.
39
40   EXAMINATION BY MR. BARBER (counsel for defendants):
41
42   Q: Mr. Shrackle, just to clarify some matters and pin it down
43   here in the deposition, what was the first indication of the
44   presence of Mrs. Potter that you had?
45
46   A: The impact.
47
48   Q: Was it a noise?
49
50
51
52

```
 1    A:   Yes.
 2
 3    Q:   Can you tell us or do you remember where the front of your
 4         vehicle was with relation to the sidewalk on the south side
 5         of Kirby when you heard that sound?
 6
 7    A:   I was in the eastern lane southbound on Kirby, or on Mattis,
 8         rather.
 9
10    Q:   And can you tell us with relation to that sidewalk where the
11         front of your vehicle was?
12
13    A:   I was south of the sidewalk, I believe.
14
15    Q:   And, when you say you were in the eastern lane, can you tell
16         us, is there a median strip?
17
18    A:   Yes.
19
20    Q:   On Mattis?
21
22    A:   Yes.
23
24    Q:   When you were south of that intersection, where was your
25         vehicle with relation to that median strip?
26
27    A:   I would say about four feet over the median strip. Perhaps a
28         little more.
29
30    Q:   Four feet to the west of it?
31
32    A:   Yes.
33
34    Q:   Where did the sound of the impact come from with relation to
35         the front part of your vehicle?
36
37    A:   Left front.
38
39    Q:   What did you do then?
40
41    A:   Applied the brakes.
42
43    Q:   When you say you applied the brakes, can--what did you do?
44
45    A:   I put force on the brake pedal.
46
47    Q:   What kind of force?
48
49    A:   As much as I could.
50
51    Q:   What did the vehicle do?
52
```

1	A:	Stopped.
2		
3	Q:	What did you do?
4		
5	A:	Jumped out.
6		
7	Q:	What did you see?
8		
9	A:	Well, after--I moved around the vehicle and saw Mrs. Potter
10		laying under the--
11		
12	Q:	How was she laying under the truck?
13		
14	A:	Almost straight, with her head under the front bumper and
15		her feet straight back.
16		
17	Q:	Was her head north or south?
18		
19	A:	South.
20		
21	Q:	Her feet were north?
22		
23	A:	Yes.
24		
25	Q:	Was her body lying in a north/south alignment with her head
26		south?
27		
28	A:	Yes.
29		
30	Q:	Was she conscious?
31		
32	A:	Yes.
33		
34	Q:	Did you speak to her?
35		
36	A:	I spoke to her.
37		
38	Q:	What did you say?
39		
40	A:	I said, "Where did you come from?"
41		
42	Q:	Did she speak to you?
43		
44	A:	No. No.
45		
46	Q:	What did you do then?
47		
48	A:	Well, the police arrived almost immediately. We got a first
49		aid kit out of my truck and applied a compress to her
50		forehead and then we waited for the ambulance to come.
51		
52	Q:	Did the truck leave skid marks?

```
1    A:   Yes.
2
3    Q:   Do you know how long they were or did someone else measure
4         them?
5
6    A:   The police measured them.
7
8    Q:   Where was your truck precisely when it stopped with relation
9         to that median strip, again? How far west of the median
10        strip was it when it stopped?
11
12   A:   I would--
13
14   Q:   If you know.
15
16   A:   I really don't know that.
17
18   Q:   Only if you know. Did you examine your truck for marks?
19
20   A:   Yes.
21
22   Q:   What did you see?
23
24 ↙ A:   There were some marks on the hood.
25
26   Q:   Where were they precisely?
27
28 ↙ A:   On the left-hand side of the hood near the division between
29        the hood and the bumper--or, the hood and the fender.
30
31   MR. BARBER (counsel for defendants):I have no other questions.
32
33   EXAMINATION BY MR. JAMES (counsel for plaintiff):
34
35   Q:   Mr. Shrackle, you mentioned a mark on the left front of the
36        truck?
37
38   A:   Yes.
39
40   Q:   Would that be the driver's side or the passenger's side?
41
42   A:   The driver's side.
43
44   Q:   Were you at the scene when the deputy coroner arrived and
45        took some photographs?
46
47   A:   Yes, sir.
48
49   (Document was thereupon marked Plaintiff's Exhibit No. 1 for
50   Identification.)
51
52
```

Potter v. Shrackle Case File

```
1    Q:   Mr. Shrackle, I hand you a photograph which has been marked
2         for purposes of identification as Plaintiff's Exhibit 1--
3
4    A:   Yes.
5
6    Q:   (Continuing)--and I would ask that you examine that. Does
7         that photograph truly and accurately depict your automobile
8         as it appeared sometime after three-thirty p.m. on the
9         afternoon of November 30, YR-2?
10
11   A:   Yes.
12
13   Q:   The position of the truck in the photograph is not in the
14        same position that it was at the time you initially stopped
15        after the impact, is that true?
16
17   A:   It should be.
18
19   Q:   All right. Was your truck moved back shortly after the
20        police or the ambulance arrived?
21
22   A:   Yes. We moved it back to--
23
24   Q:   Was the photograph taken before or after it was moved back?
25
26   A:   I can't honestly say.
27
28   MR. BARBER (counsel for defendants): If you don't know, say you
29        don't know. That is the answer.
30
31   A:   I don't know.
32
33   MR. JAMES (counsel for plaintiff): I would call your attention to
34        some dark splotches on the pavement just in front--
35
36   MR. BARBER (counsel for defendants): I don't think there will be
37        any contest. It's obvious to me they moved the car back.
38        Mrs. Potter isn't under it and I see the blood marks on the
39        pavement, too,and I know the officer will testify that they
40        are blood stains.
41
42   MR. JAMES (counsel for plaintiff): All right. Do you recall, Mr.
43        Shrackle, whether the wheels on your truck were moved as
44        your truck was pushed back?
45
46   A:   I don't recall.
47
48   Q:   You mentioned that as soon as you heard the thud, you
49        applied the brakes. Was your foot on the accelerator at the
50        time you heard the impact?
51
52
```

```
 1   A:    I would--I could not say for sure.
 2
 3   Q:    Was it on the brake at the time you heard the impact?
 4
 5   MR. BARBER (counsel for defendants): Tell him what your best
 6         recollection is.
 7
 8   A:    My best recollection is it was on the brake.
 9
10   Q:    Do you recall why it would have been on the brake at the
11         time you heard the impact?
12
13   A:    Because I was going around the corner and I would have-- my
14         best recollection is it was on the brake simply as a
15         precaution when you go around the corner.
16
17   Q:    I believe you testified that the front of your vehicle was
18         south of the sidewalk at the time you first heard the
19         impact, is that correct?
20
21   A:    To the best of my recollection.
22
23   MR. JAMES (counsel for plaintiff): I have no further questions.
24
25   MR. BARBER (counsel for defendants): Thank you, Mr. Shrackle.
26
27   This deposition was taken in the office of plaintiff's counsel on
28   June 19, YR-1. After the deposition was transcribed, it was
29   signed by the deponent, Charles T. Shrackle.
30
31
32   Certified by
33
34
35
36   _Paula J. Brooks_____
37   Paula Brooks
38   Certified Shorthand Reporter
39   (CSR)
```

DEPOSITION OF JEFFREY POTTER*

I am thirty-two years of age. I'm an assistant professor in the physics department at the University of Nita. I received a bachelor's degree in physics from Purdue and a doctorate in physics from the University of Wisconsin/Madison. I received my Ph.D. five years ago and have been at the University of Nita since then.

Katherine and I were married eight years ago. We met while both of us were attending Purdue University in Indiana. I graduated from Purdue and went to graduate school at the University of Wisconsin/Madison. We continued to date, and then were married the summer before Katherine's junior year in college. Katherine continued her college education at the University of Wisconsin while I was in graduate school. Katherine received her bachelor's degree in mathematics from the University of Wisconsin and a master's degree in mathematics from the University of Nita. She was finishing the course work for her doctorate at the time of her death. Katherine was 28 years old when she died.

While doing her graduate work at the University of Nita, Katherine also was working as a mathematician in computer science. She was employed by the university in a computer science group called the Advanced Computation Conference. She was in charge of the linear programming work done on a new computer the group was building, the Nitae III. She hoped to continue working with the ACC group after getting her doctorate in computer science. Once she received her degree, however, she would probably have received many offers, both in academia and industry, as persons with her background are very much in demand.

Katherine and I had no children. We had decided to wait until Katherine had completed her doctorate before making a decision about a family. We had a "fifty-fifty equal partnership" marriage. All of our income was pooled and we shared household chores equally.

---

*The transcript of Jeffrey Potter's deposition was excerpted so that only his answers are reprinted here. Assume that this is a true and accurate rendering of those answers.

This deposition was taken in the office of defendant's counsel on September 19, YR-1. After the deposition was transcribed, it was signed by the deponent.

Certified by

Anne Dolan

Anne Dolan
Certified Shorthand Reporter
(CSR)

DEPOSITION OF DANIEL SLOAN*

I am forty-two years of age. I am Professor of Computer Science at the University of Nita, where I also am the Director of the Advanced Computation Conference, which is a group working on new computer applications.

I have a B.S. and a M.S. degree from Columbia University and a Ph.D. from New York University, all in applied mathematics. Before coming to the university, I was in industry for ten years with Westinghouse and IBM, including a period as manager of Westinghouse's advanced development in its aero-space division. I am a member of the Institute of Electrical and Aeronautical Engineers. In 1975, I was selected for the Federation of Information Processing Society's annual prize for outstanding work in the field of computer science.

The Advanced Computation Conference (ACC) is an interdisciplinary research unit concentrating on applications of the computer. As director, I am responsible for the management of the center, including personnel. I am active in the recruitment of personnel, and in my capacity as a university professor, in the placement of personnel. I have been director of the ACC for three and one-half years. Before that I was director of the Nitae III computer project, a predecessor research group.

I had known Katherine Potter professionally for five years. I was her supervisor during her employment on both the Nitae III project and the ACC project. Mrs. Potter began as a research assistant and progressed to research programmer and then to senior research programmer. She worked only part-time once she resumed her graduate studies.

My opinion of Katherine Potter's work was very high. I would have hired her to work with the ACC project once she had obtained her doctorate. Upon completion of her doctorate, Katherine could have started at a salary of at least $30,000 in an academic position or a minimum of $40,000 in an industry position.

Katherine Potter's work on her Ph.D. was progressing satisfactorily at the time of her death, and in my opinion, she would have received her doctorate degree within one and one-half years (i.e., May YR-0), or at the latest two years (i.e., December YR-0), had she not been killed.

---

*The transcript of Daniel Sloan's deposition was excerpted so that only his answers are reprinted here. Assume that this is a true and accurate rendering of those answers.

1
2
3
4
5
6
7
8
9
10
11
12
13

This deposition was taken in the office of defendant's counsel on August 17, YR-1. After the deposition was transcribed, it was signed by the deponent.

Certified by

Anne Dolan
Anne Dolan
Certified Shorthand Reporter
(CSR)

ECONOMIC ANALYSIS

REPORT RE: KATHERINE POTTER*

Prepared by

Robert Glenn
Professor of Economics
University of Nita
Nita City, Nita

July 1, YR-1

*This report was prepared by Dr. Roger Skurski, Department of Economics, the University of Notre Dame, and Fred S. McChesney, J.D., Ph.D., consultant on Expert Testimony, Emory University School of Law. NITA expresses its appreciation to Dr. Skurski and Dr. McChesney for their preparation of these materials. The economic data in this report was updated in March 1990.

TABLE I

SUMMARY OF ECONOMIC LOSSES
KATHERINE POTTER, AGE 28 TO 60

Date of Birth: 4/23/YR-30 *Date of Death:* 11/30/YR-2, Age 28

Appraisal Period: YR-1 to YR+30, 32 years *Projected Retirement:*
Age 60, YR+30 *1/*

		Academic	Industry
A.	Future Earnings *2/* (YR-1 to YR+30)	$3,475,124	$ 3,792,089
B.	Future Fringe Benefits *3/* (YR-1 to YR+30)	615,097	758,104
C.	Personal Consumption *4/* (76.4% of A)	2,654,995	2,897,156
D.	Future Value of Household Work *5/*	1,219,013	1,219,013
E.	Subtotal (A+B-C+D)	2,654,239	2,872,050
F.	Net Present Value of Loss *6/*	519,774	578,163

1/ Projected retirement at age 60 is a conservative estimate as most individuals work beyond age 60, particularly in Mrs. Potter's field. Such a conservative projection, however, has built in latitude for absences from the labor market for such things as child bearing and rearing and illness. It is assumed Mrs. Potter would finish out the academic or work year in which she turned 60.

2/ See Table II.

3/ See Table V.

4/ See Table VI and Application of Table VI to Potter Household.

5/ See Table VII.

6/ See note 4, Table II.

TABLE II

PROSPECTIVE INCOME STREAM OF KATHERINE POTTER
IN ACADEMIC AND INDUSTRIAL EMPLOYMENT
FROM AGE 28 TO 60

Date of Birth:	4/23/YR-30	*Date of Death:*	12/4/YR-2, Age 28
Appraisal Period:	YR-1 - YR+30, 32 years	*Projected Retirement:*	Age 60, YR+30

YEAR	FUTURE INCOME			PRESENT DISCOUNTED VALUE AT YR-0 4/	
	Acad. *1/*	Ind. *2/*		Acad.	Ind.
YR-1	$ 6,563 *3/*	$ 6,563 *3/*		$ 6,563	$ 6,563
YR-0	7,095	7,095		7,095	7,095
YR+1	30,000	40,000		27,372	36,496
YR+2	32,430	42,800		26,998	35,631
YR+3	35,057	45,796		26,628	34,785
YR+4	37,896	49,002		26,264	33,960
YR+5	40,966	52,432		25,904	33,154
YR+6	44,284	56,102		25,550	32,368
YR+7	47,871	60,029		25,200	31,600
YR+8	51,749	64,231		24,855	30,850
YR+9	55,941	68,727		24,515	30,119
YR+10	60,472	73,538		24,179	29,404
YR+11	65,370	78,686		23,849	28,707
YR+12	70,665	84,194		23,522	28,026
YR+13	76,389	90,088		23,200	27,361
YR+14	82,576	96,394		22,883	26,712
YR+15	89,265	103,141		22,570	26,078
YR+16	96,495	110,361		22,261	25,459
YR+17	104,312	118,087		21,956	24,855
YR+18	112,761	126,353		21,655	24,266
YR+19	121,894	135,197		21,359	23,690
YR+20	131,768	144,661		21,067	23,128
YR+21	142,441	154,787		20,778	22,579
YR+22	153,979	165,622		20,494	22,044
YR+23	166,451	177,216		20,214	21,521
YR+24	179,934	189,621		19,937	21,010
YR+25	194,508	202,895		19,664	20,512
YR+26	210,263	217,097		19,395	20,025
YR+27	227,295	232,294		19,130	19,550
YR+28	245,706	248,555		18,868	19,087
YR+29	265,608	265,954		18,609	18,634
YR+30	287,122	284,570		18,355	18,192
TOTALS *5/*	**$3,475,124**	**$3,792,089**		**$690,888**	**$803,461**

Notes follow on the next page.

NOTES FOR TABLE II

1/   Projected at an 8.1% annual rate of increase based on current averages for college teachers nationwide as presented in *Academe* (Bulletin of the American Association of University Professors), April YR-1, p. 265. *See* Table III.

2/   Projected at a 7.0% annual rate of increase based on the YR-12-YR-2 average increase in earnings and compensation in the business sector of the economy as given by the U.S. Bureau of Labor Statistics, reported in the Statistical Abstract of the United States YR-1, Table 699. *See* Table IV.

3/   Arrived at by working one-quarter time for three quarters of the year and one-half time for one quarter of the year at an annual salary of $21,000. Information about Katherine Potter's rate of pay at the time of her death, and her projected starting salary in academic and industrial positions (YR-1) was obtained from Dr. Daniel Sloan of the University of Nita.

4/   Discounted at 9.6%, the average annual yield on long-term U.S. government bonds over the last ten years. Statistical Abstract, Table 856. This rate (9.6%) represents the rate of return a person could expect on investments with virtually no risk. If interest rates should rise above this in the future, wage and salary growth will also rise, and thus the present discounted values presented here will remain essentially unchanged. The key here is the difference between the growth in compensation and the discount rate: 8.1% - 9.6% = -1.5% had Mrs. Potter pursued an academic career and 7.0% - 9.6% = 2.6% had she taken the industrial route. Therefore, her *real income* would have suffered an annual decline of 1.5 percent in the first case or experienced a decline of 2.6 percent in the second, and either one of these is quite conservative.

5/   Totals may not equal the component sums due to rounding.

TABLE III

PERCENTAGE INCREASES IN SALARY FOR FACULTY ON STAFF FOR BOTH YR-4 THROUGH YR-3 AND YR-3 THROUGH YR-2, BY CATEGORY, TYPE OF AFFILIATION, AND ACADEMIC RANK *1/*

ACADEMIC RANK	ALL COMBINED	PUBLIC	PRIVATE INDEPENDENT	CHURCH-RELATED
CATEGORY I *2/*				
Professor	8.1%	8.3%	7.5%	7.7%
Associate	8.4	8.4	8.5	7.9
Assistant	8.9	8.9	9.0	8.5
Instructor	8.8	8.8	8.5	9.1
All Ranks	**8.4**	**8.5**	**8.0**	**8.1**
CATEGORY IIA				
Professor	7.4	7.3	7.7	7.6
Associate	8.0	7.9	8.2	8.2
Assistant	8.6	8.5	8.7	8.7
Instructor	9.0	9.0	9.7	8.2
All Ranks	**8.1**	**8.0**	**8.2**	**8.1**
CATEGORY IIB				
Professor	7.4	7.3	7.5	7.2
Associate	8.0	8.1	8.0	7.8
Assistant	8.5	8.7	8.5	8.3
Instructor	8.8	9.0	8.8	8.5
All Ranks	**8.0**	**8.2**	**8.0**	**7.9**
CATEGORY III				
Professor	6.4	6.4	7.3	6.0
Associate	7.5	7.4	9.7%	7.7
Assistant	8.0	8.0	8.4	7.8
Instructor	8.7	8.7	8.0	8.2
All Ranks	**7.7**	**7.7**	**8.5**	**7.4**
CATEGORY IV				
No Rank	8.6	8.6	8.2	8.3
ALL CATEGORIES EXCEPT IV				
Professor	7.8	7.9	7.6	7.4
Associate	8.2	8.2	8.3	8.0
Assistant	8.7	8.7	8.7	8.5
Instructor	8.9	8.9	9.0	8.5
All Ranks	**8.1**	**8.1**	**8.1**	**8.0**

Notes follow on the next page.

NOTES FOR TABLE III

1/   Sample includes 2,214 institutions.

2/   Category I includes institutions that offer doctorate degrees and that conferred in the most recent three years an annual average of fifteen or more doctorates covering a minimum of three nonrelated disciplines. Category IIA includes institutions awarding degrees above the baccalaureate but not included in Category I. Category IIB includes institutions awarding only the baccalaureate or equivalent degree. Category III includes two-year institutions with academic ranks. Category IV includes institutions without academic ranks. (With the exception of a few liberal arts colleges, this category includes mostly two-year institutions.)

Source: Academe, April YR-1, pp. 265-85.

Potter v. Shrackle Case File

TABLE IV

ANNUAL CHANGES IN EARNINGS AND COMPENSATION PER HOUR IN THE PRIVATE BUSINESS SECTOR

YEAR	PERCENT CHANGE
YR-12	6.8
YR-11	7.3
YR-10	8.0
YR-9	8.4
YR-8	8.3
YR-7	8.1
YR-6	8.9
YR-5	5.9
YR-4	4.4
YR-3	3.9
Average	**7.0**

Source: Statistical Abstract of the United States, YR-2, Table 699.

TABLE V

FRINGE BENEFIT STREAM OF KATHERINE POTTER

YEAR	FUTURE FRINGE BENEFITS		PRESENT DISCOUNTED VALUE FRINGE BENEFITS AT YR-0 3/	
	Acad. *1/*	Ind. *2/*	Acad.	Ind.
YR-1	$ 1,162	$ 1,162	$ 1,162	$ 1,162
YR-0	1,256	1,256	1,256	1,256
YR+1	5,310	8,000	4,845	7,299
YR+2	5,740	8,560	4,779	7,126
YR+3	6,205	9,159	4,713	6,957
YR+4	6,708	9,800	4,649	6,792
YR+5	7,251	10,486	4,585	6,631
YR+6	7,838	11,220	4,522	6,474
YR+7	8,473	12,006	4,460	6,320
YR+8	9,160	12,846	4,399	6,170
YR+9	9,901	13,745	4,339	6,024
YR+10	10,703	14,708	4,280	5,881
YR+11	11,570	15,737	4,221	5,741
YR+12	12,508	16,839	4,163	5,605
YR+13	13,521	18,018	4,106	5,472
YR+14	14,616	19,279	4,050	5,342
YR+15	15,800	20,628	3,995	5,216
YR+16	17,080	22,072	3,940	5,092
YR+17	18,463	23,617	3,886	4,971
YR+18	19,959	25,271	3,833	4,853
YR+19	21,575	27,039	3,781	4,738
YR+20	23,323	28,932	3,729	4,626
YR+21	25,212	30,957	3,678	4,516
YR+22	27,254	33,124	3,627	4,409
YR+23	29,462	35,443	3,578	4,304
YR+24	31,848	37,924	3,529	4,202
YR+25	34,428	40,579	3,481	4,102
YR+26	37,217	43,419	3,433	4,005
YR+27	40,231	46,459	3,386	3,910
YR+28	43,490	49,711	3,340	3,817
YR+29	47,013	53,191	3,294	3,727
YR+30	50,821	56,914	3,249	3,638
TOTAL *4/*	**$ 615,097**	**$758,104**	**$122,287**	**$160,378**

Notes follow on the next page.

NOTES FOR TABLE V

1/   Future fringe benefits are computed in the academic sphere as 17.7% of the future income for each year of Mrs. Potter's expected worklife. *See Academe*, April YR-1, p. 272.

2/   Except for YR-1 and YR-0 when the academic rate of 17.7% is used, future fringe benefits are computed in the industrial sphere as 20.0% of the future income for each year of Mrs. Potter's expected worklife. *See* U.S. Bureau of Labor Statistics, *Handbook of Labor Statistics* (Washington: U.S. Government Printing Office, YR-3), p. 237.

3/   Discounted to present value at 9.6%. See footnote 4/ to Table II for further information.

4/   Totals may not sum due to rounding.

TABLE VI

SUMMARY OF FAMILY EXPENDITURES, INCOME, AND SAVINGS, FOR FAMILY WITH INCOME OF $30,000 OR MORE, YR-2

	AVERAGE, IN DOLLARS	PERCENTAGE OF MONEY INCOME
Money Income, before taxes	$ 44,152	100%
Taxes	6,684	15%
Money Income, after taxes	37,441	85%
Current Consumption	30,338	69%
(Housing Expenditures)	8,492	19%
(Personal Insurance)	570	0.1%
(Case Contributions)	1,209	3%
Savings	7,103	16%

Source: U.S. Bureau of Labor Statistics, *Consumer Expenditures Survey: Interview Survey YR-2*, published in April, YR-1.

Potter v. Shrackle Case File

APPLICATION OF TABLE VI TO POTTER HOUSEHOLD

The deceased Katherine Potter's net contribution to household welfare (i.e., what Jeffrey Potter will lose monetarily as a result of his wife's death) will consist of:

1. Her contributions to savings,
2. Her gifts and other contributions, and
3. One-half of the housing expenditures.

Based on the information contained in Table VI, savings will average 16% of income, gifts and contributions will average 3.1% of income, and one-half of housing expenditures will average 9.5% of income.

Therefore, the total income available to the household's discretionary use in any given year will average 28.6% of the decedent's income. This figure may be reduced to 23.6% if allowance is made for domestic help.

If the 23.6% figure is used as the deceased Katherine Potter's projected contribution to the household welfare, her projected income, discounted to present value, should be reduced by 76.4% in order to project the net losses to her husband, Jeffrey Potter, caused by her death.

TABLE VII

PROJECTED VALUE OF HOUSEHOLD ACTIVITIES OF
KATHERINE POTTER FROM AGE 28 TO 60

YEAR	FUTURE VALUES 2/	PRESENT DISCOUNTED VALUE AT YR-0 3/
YR-1	$ 11,060 *1/*	$ 11,060
YR-0	11,834	11,834
YR+1	12,663	11,553
YR+2	13,549	11,279
YR+3	14,497	11,012
YR+4	15,512	10,751
YR+5	16,598	10,496
YR+6	17,760	10,247
YR+7	19,003	10,003
YR+8	20,333	9,766
YR+9	21,757	9,534
YR+10	23,280	9,308
YR+11	24,909	9,087
YR+12	26,653	8,872
YR+13	28,519	8,661
YR+14	30,515	8,456
YR+15	32,651	8,255
YR+16	34,936	8,060
YR+17	37,382	7,868
YR+18	39,999	7,682
YR+19	42,799	7,499
YR+20	45,795	7,322
YR+21	49,000	7,148
YR+22	52,430	6,978
YR+23	56,100	6,813
YR+24	60,027	
6,651		
YR+25	64,229	6,493
YR+26	68,725	6,339
YR+27	73,536	6,189
YR+28	78,684	6,042
YR+29	84,192	5,899
YR+30	90,085	5,759
TOTAL 4/	**$1,219,013**	**$272,918**

Notes follow on the next page.

NOTES FOR TABLE VII

1/   Based on data collected from almost 1,400 families on their expenditure of time on household operations (*see* Kathryn E. Walker and William H. Gauger, *The Dollar Value of Household Work, Consumer Economics and Public Policy Bulletin,* No. 5, Cornell University, p. 6) and information about the Potter family, it is assumed that a working wife such as Katherine Potter would on the average spend three hours per day on household work. The value of Mrs. Potter's time presently is $10.10 per hour as a computer specialist ($21,000/2080 hours; *see* Table II, Note 3). Although when she completes her Ph.D. and begins teaching or doing industrial research, her time will be worth much more; we employ $10.10 throughout her expected worklife. Thus, $10.10/hr x 3 hrs/day x 365 days/yr. = $11,060.

2/   Projected at the same 7.0% employed earlier. *See* Table II, Note 2.

3/   Discounted at 9.6%. *See* Table II, Note 4.

4/   Due to rounding, items may not sum to total.

BIOGRAPHICAL INFORMATION ABOUT ROBERT W. GLENN*

Present Position: Professor of Economics
University of Nita
Nita City, Nita

Education: B.S., Economics, University of North Carolina, YR-18
Ph.D., Economics, University of Illinois, YR-14

Teaching: Taught economics at the undergraduate and graduate level at the University of Nita for fourteen years. Taught at numerous seminars in industry.

Research: Directed graduate research.
Research and publication in economic journals.
Received research grants from the National Science Foundation, the Social Science Research Council, the Center for Comparative Studies at the University of Nita, and the Nita Law Enforcement Commission.

---

*If an actual economist plays the role of Dr. Glenn, the credentials of the person playing the role should be substituted for those stated here.

NITA STATE UNIVERSITY

DEPARTMENT OF ECONOMICS   **ELIZABETH C. BUCHANAN, PH.D.**

September 1, YR-1

Pierce, Johnson and Clark
Nita National Bank Plaza
Nita City, Nita 99994

Ladies and Gentlemen:

This is in response to your recent letter asking for my professional analysis of the "Report Re: Katherine Potter" prepared by Dr. Robert W. Glenn, Professor of Economics, University of Nita. I believe that Professor Glenn's opinion is subject to criticism on a number of bases. I begin with criticisms of several of Dr. Glenn's assumptions and of the quality of his data.

First, Dr. Glenn assumes that Mrs. Potter would have completed her Ph.D. degree and entered the labor force in two years. My own experience with graduate students is that one can never be so confident. Delays often occur. Indeed, there is nothing in Dr. Glenn's report to support his judgment that Mrs. Potter was making satisfactory progress toward her degree, enjoyed her program, would have desired to complete the degree, and so on.

Second, Dr. Glenn assumes that Mrs. Potter would have retired at age 60. That again is an assumption as to which no economist is an expert. Dr. Glenn's report is no more accurate than the validity of this utterly intestable proposition.

Third, Dr. Glenn qualifies the age 60 assumption by saying that such an assumption compensates for the fact that Mrs. Potter might have been out of the labor force for some period of time prior to the date of her actual retirement if that retirement occurred beyond age 60. Quite apart from reiterating that Mrs. Potter might have retired before or after the date Dr. Glenn assumed, the assumption ignores the fact that one cannot substitute a year away from the labor force early in one's career for a year out of the labor force later in the career. That is, the present value of Mrs. Potter's earnings in her child-bearing years can be seen on Dr. Glenn's own tables to be different than the present value of her earnings at the end of her career. Unfortunately for your case, however, Dr. Glenn's assumption tends to understate the loss to Mr. Potter, because the present value of her salary in the future is shown as lower than the present value of salary in her child-bearing years.

Fourth, Dr. Glenn's projections of salary increases, whether in academic or industrial positions, are based on data from relatively recent years which cannot fairly be said to establish a trend that will apply over the next thirty years. That is to say, the projections average a period of extreme inflation in this country in the 1970s with a recent period of unusual price stability. To project wages as increasing at a rate of 7% or 8.1% annually, then, is to make a pretense of scientific rationality out of what is a wild, unjustified guess. Indeed, one need only look at Dr. Glenn's conclusion that by YR+30 academic mathematicians will be making more than mathematicians in industry to realize that Dr. Glenn's assumptions are unreasonable.

Fifth, the same criticism can be made with respect to the discount rate which Dr. Glenn has chosen since the interest rate is made up of a variety of factors such as inflationary expectations and budget deficits that almost certainly will not be present in each or even most of the next 30 years. The discount rate of 9.6%, even assuming it were composed of the right elements, then, would be too high, but since a higher than proper rate would tend to understate the present value of Mrs. Potter's lifetime earnings, I expect that this is one way in which Dr. Glenn's report can fairly be said to be "conservative."

Having made all of the above observations one must come away with the conclusion that none of them individually or taken together are likely to do substantial damage to Dr. Glenn's overall conclusion. That is, the same factors that make Dr. Glenn's estimates of wage increases too high also would tend to make the appropriate discount rate much higher. Thus, Dr. Glenn is probably right that the difference between the rate of growth in wages and the appropriate discount rate (what Dr. Glenn calls the change in "real income") is probably quite small. Indeed, while I believe that his projected *decline* in real income of 1.5 to 2.6% is probably wrong, it is wrong in a way that *reduces* the damages to which Mr. Potter would be entitled. Thus, attacking this finding is probably not in your interest.

In five other areas, however, Dr. Glenn has made assumptions that can make a dramatic difference in the conclusion as to the economic loss suffered by Mr. Potter.

First, Dr. Glenn has attributed to Mrs. Potter a $1.22 million value on her future household work. This is based on the assumption that she would have worked three hours each day on housework and that the value of that work was the value of her time as a computer specialist, namely $10.10 per hour.

Initially, this assumption that the value of her time should be measured by her alternative use of time in computer work is highly doubtful. It seems that any reasonable economist would use instead the cost to the family of hiring someone for three hours a day to do domestic work. The minimum wage is presently less than 35% of the figure used by Dr. Glenn. At minimum, then, reducing Dr. Glenn's estimate of the value of her household work by two-thirds would seem extremely conservative.

In fact, it seems that this "housework" factor should not be included in measuring Mr. Potter's loss at all. The Potters were a couple who shared housekeeping responsibilities. It seems appropriate to assume that Mr. Potter would have a need for a smaller housing unit when he is living alone than he had prior to Mrs. Potter's death. Under these circumstances, and recognizing that unmarried men frequently do their own housekeeping chores, it seems that the loss of Mrs. Potter's services in doing her half of the household work would be so speculative as to be inappropriate for inclusion in the damage calculations. And lest one think that removal of this item would be relatively insignificant, a quick glance at Dr. Glenn's Table I reveals that the future value of household work represents almost 50% of the total recovery sought by Mr. Potter. Removal of this item from the calculation would thus reduce Mr. Potter's present loss by over $270,000.

Second, Dr. Glenn assumes that gifts and contributions made by Mrs. Potter were a contribution to family well being which would constitute a "loss" to Mr. Potter. I see no basis for concluding that that is the case at all. The fact that Mrs. Potter (or any other hypothetical person in the category described in Table 6) would decide to give a particular portion of her income to the Red Cross, for example, would not mean that her husband would conclude that he had to make up for that expenditure after her death. All this is to say that while the loss of income with which Mrs. Potter might have made contributions might constitute a loss to those charities who might have received the gifts, they are not a loss fairly said to be suffered by Mr. Potter.

Third, the conclusion that Mr. Potter would be denied one-half of Mrs. Potter's expenditures on housing (i.e., 10% of her total income) is similarly excessive. One cannot assume that Mr. Potter would stay in precisely the same kind of housing accommodations when he did not have a spouse. His savings might not be one-half of the housing expenditure before Mrs. Potter's death, but I think that, at the outside, his loss of contribution toward housing is more like 5% than 10% of Mrs. Potter's income.

Fourth, Dr. Glenn has assumed that the future fringe benefits which Mrs. Potter would have received are entirely a net loss to Mr. Potter. This seems totally inaccurate. Fringe benefits are uniquely personal to the recipient and difficult to transfer to a spouse or others. One might say, for example, that dependent medical coverage is an exception to my assertion, but most fringe benefits such as vacation, social security contributions, employee health insurance and the like, are things which Mr. Potter could not have enjoyed during Mrs. Potter's lifetime and the loss of which is not something for which he should be compensated at all.

Thus, if I am correct that Mr. Potter's real loss in this case consists of the 5% of her income that Mrs. Potter would have contributed toward housing and the 8% that she might have contributed to savings, that means Mr. Potter's loss would be 13% of Mrs. Potter's projected income, not 24%. Dr. Glenn on Table I concludes that the total figure which he must reduce to present value over thirty years is $2.65 million. If I am right as to each of the preceding five major items of deduction, then that figure would be reduced to $450,000.

Applying the formulas which Dr. Glenn used to reduce that figure to present value, the conclusion as to the net present value of Mr. Potter's loss is not the $691,000 to $803,000 that Dr. Glenn concluded, but rather $90,000 to $104,000.

There is always a tendency for an analysis such as mine to sound hard-hearted and an analysis such as Dr. Glenn's to seem more "humane." The economic reality is, however, that most of us consume a substantial portion of what we produce over our lifetimes. The net economic loss from our demise is less than we, and life insurance salesmen who play upon our vanity, would like to think.

Respectfully submitted,

Elizabeth C. Buchanan

Elizabeth C. Buchanan, Ph.D.
Professor of Economics
Nita State University

APPLICABLE NITA STATUTES

Motor Vehicles — Chapter 89

Section 12(4). Right of Way. Public Roadways. Negligence

A. *Motor Vehicles.* The driver of a motor vehicle shall yield the right of way, by slowing down or stopping if necessary, to a pedestrian crossing the roadway within a crosswalk when the pedestrian is upon that half of the roadway in which the vehicle is traveling, or when either the vehicle or the pedestrian is approaching that half of the roadway so closely that the pedestrian is in danger.

B. *Pedestrian.* A pedestrian crossing a roadway at any point other than within a marked crosswalk shall yield the right of way to all vehicles upon the roadway.

C. *Negligence.* This right of way, however, is not absolute, but rather creates a duty upon the party having the right of way to exercise ordinary care to avoid collisions.

Wrongful Death — Chapter 70

Section 1. Liability

Whenever the death of a person shall be caused by wrongful act, neglect, or default, and the act, neglect, or default is such as would, if death had not ensued, have entitled the party injured to maintain an action and recover damages in respect thereof, then, and in every such case, the person who or company or corporation which would have been liable if death had not ensued, shall be liable to an action for damages, notwithstanding the death of the person injured, and although the death shall have been caused under such circumstances as amount in law to a felony.

Section 2. Damages

A. Damages recoverable for death by wrongful act include:

1. Expenses for care, treatment, and hospitalization incident to the injury resulting in death;

2. Compensation for pain and suffering of the decedent;

3. The reasonable funeral expenses of the decedent;

4. The present monetary value of the decedent to the persons entitled to receive the damages recovered, including but not limited to compensation for the loss of the reasonable expected

   (a) net income of the decedent,
   (b) services, protection, care, and assistance of the decedent, whether voluntary or obligatory, to the persons entitled to the damages recovered,
   (c) society, companionship, comfort, guidance, kindly offices, and advice of the decedent to the persons entitled to the damages recovered;

5. Such punitive damages as the decedent could have recovered had he or she survived, and the punitive damages for wrongfully causing the death of the decedent through malice, willful or wanton injury, or gross negligence;

6. Nominal damages when the jury so finds.

B. All evidence which reasonably tends to establish any of the elements of damages included in subsection A, or otherwise reasonably tends to establish the present monetary value of the decedent to the persons entitled to receive the damages recovered, is admissible in an action for damages for death by wrongful act.

Comparative Negligence — Chapter 140

Section 3. Contributory Negligence No Bar to Recovery of Damages

In all action hereafter brought for personal injuries, or where such injuries have resulted in death, or for injury to property, the fact that the person injured, or the owner of the property, or the person having control over the property may have been guilty of contributory negligence shall not bar a recovery, but damages shall be diminished by the jury in proportion to the amount of negligence attributable to the person injured, or the owner of the property, or the person having control over the property.

PROPOSED JURY INSTRUCTIONS[*]

1.   The Court will now instruct you on the claims and defenses of each party and the law governing the case. You must arrive at your verdict by unanimous vote, applying the law, as you are now instructed, to the facts as you find them to be.

2.   The parties to this case are Jeffrey Potter, both individually in his own behalf and as administrator of Katherine Potter's estate, as plaintiff against defendants Charles T. Shrackle and the Shrackle Construction Company.

3.   Defendants have admitted in the pleadings, and you must regard as conclusively proven the following:

- Katherine Potter died on December 4, YR-2.
- Plaintiff Jeffrey Potter and the decedent, Katherine Potter, were married at the time of her death and had been married for eight years.
- Plaintiff Jeffrey Potter has been duly appointed the administrator of Katherine Potter's estate.
- On November 30, YR-2, at around 3:30 P.M., Katherine Potter was crossing Mattis Street when she was struck by a pickup truck driven by Charles T. Shrackle and owned by the Shrackle Construction Company. Katherine Potter was seriously injured, and she died on December 4, YR-2 as a result of those injuries.

4.   Plaintiff claims that Charles Shrackle was negligent in his operation and control of the pickup truck and that his negligence caused Katherine Potter's injuries and death. Plaintiff seeks damages for defendants' negligence both on behalf of himself individually and as the administrator of Katherine Potter's estate. Thus, plaintiff has brought this lawsuit and is claiming damages in two separate capacities: (1) as an individual for the injury and loss suffered by him as Katherine Potter's husband, and (2) as the administrator of Katherine Potter's estate for the pain, suffering, and expenses in incurred by her prior to her death.

   Defendants deny that Charles Shrackle was negligent or that his negligence caused Katherine Potter's injuries and death. Defendants claim that Katherine Potter was negligent, and that it was her own negligence that caused her injuries and death.

---

[*]*These proposed instructions are applicable to this case only. They are borrowed or adapted from California, Missouri, and Washington pattern jury instructions. For general jury instructions, see those set forth after these instructions.*

5. In this case, the plaintiff, Jeffrey Potter, has the burden of proving:

    (1) That Charles Shrackle was negligent, and

    (2) That the negligence of Charles Shrackle proximately caused Katherine Potter's death.

    The defendants have the burden of proving:

    (1) That the deceased, Katherine Potter, was contributorily negligent, and

    (2) That the contributory negligence of Katherine Potter proximately caused her death.

    Thus, each of the parties to this case has a burden of proof to maintain, and you are to determine whether they have met their burdens. Your task is to determine whether Charles Shrackle or Katherine Potter, or both, were negligent, and the extent to which their negligence caused Katherine Potter's injuries and death.

6. *Negligence.* The terms "negligent" or "negligence" as used in these instructions mean the failure to use that degree of care that an ordinarily careful and prudent person would use under the same or similar circumstances.

7. *Contributory Negligence.* The terms "contributorily negligent" or "contributory negligence" mean negligence on the part of the deceased Katherine Potter.

8. *Duty of Driver and Pedestrian.* It is the duty of every person using a public street or highway, whether a pedestrian or a driver of a vehicle, to exercise ordinary care to avoid placing himself or others in danger and to exercise ordinary care to avoid a collision.

9. *Violation of a Statute.* The violation of a statute, if you find any, is negligence as a matter of law. Such negligence has the same effect as any other act or acts of negligence.

    A statute in the state of Nita provides:

    (1) That the driver of a motor vehicle shall yield the right of way, by slowing down or stopping if necessary, to a pedestrian crossing the roadway within a crosswalk when the pedestrian is upon that half of the roadway in which the vehicle is traveling, or when either the vehicle or the pedestrian is approaching that half of the roadway so closely that the pedestrian is in danger.

(2) That a pedestrian crossing a roadway at any point other than within a marked crosswalk shall yield the right of way to all vehicles upon the roadway.

(3) This right of way, however, is not absolute but rather creates a duty to exercise ordinary care to avoid collisions upon the party having the right of way.

10. *Proximate Cause.* Proximate cause is that cause which, in a natural and continuous sequence, produces the injury, and without which the injury would not have occurred.

To be a proximate cause of Katherine Potter's injuries and death, negligent conduct by either Charles Shrackle or Katherine Potter need not be the only cause,nor the last or nearest cause. It is sufficient if the negligent conduct acting concurrently with another cause produced the injury.

Thus, there need not be only one proximate cause of Katherine Potter's injuries and death, and you may find that the negligence of both Charles Shrackle and Katherine Potter was the proximate cause of her death. On the other hand, you may find that the negligence of either of them was the sole proximate cause of her death.

11. *Comparative Negligence.* In the state of Nita, we have what is called a "pure comparative negligence" statute. The statute provides, as here pertinent:

> In all actions hereafter brought for personal injuries, or where such injuries have resulted in death, . . . the fact that the person injured . . . may have been guilty of contributory negligence shall not bar a recovery, but damages shall be diminished by the jury in proportion to the amount of negligence attributable to the person injured . . . .

What this means is that the contributory negligence of Katherine Potter, if any, would not bar the plaintiff's recovery. The statute directs you to apportion the responsibility and, thus, the damages in accordance with the relative fault of the parties. Therefore, the damages allowed to be recovered by the plaintiff should be diminished in proportion to the amount of negligence which was a legal cause of the deceased's death and which was attributed to the deceased, whether or not such negligence is greater than that of the defendant.

12. *Findings of Negligence — Percentage.* You are to determine the negligence, if any, of both Charles Shrackle and Katherine Potter, and then to apportion the responsibility of each.

Please state your findings of negligence in the following form:

We find the conduct of the defendant, Charles Shrackle, was _____% negligent.

We find that the conduct of the deceased, Katherine Potter, was _____% negligent.

13. *Liability of the Shrackle Construction Company.* A company is responsible for the acts of persons acting on its behalf and for its benefit and purpose.

You are to determine in this case whether Charles Shrackle was performing duties for or acting on behalf of the construction company at the time Katherine Potter was struck. If you find that Charles Shrackle was acting within the scope of the construction company's business at the time of the incident, then the company is liable for his acts; however, if you find that he was not acting within the scope of the construction company's business at the time, then the company has not liability in this case whatsoever.

14. *Damages.* In this case you must also decide the issue of damages. You must determine the amount which will reasonably and fairly compensate Jeffrey Potter for the losses resulting from the death of his wife, Katherine Potter.

In determining the loss to the plaintiff, Jeffrey Potter, you should consider the following factors:

(1) Expenses for care, treatment, and hospitalization incident to the injury to Katherine Potter resulting in her death;

(2) Compensation for the pain and suffering of the decedent;

(3) The reasonable funeral expenses of the decedent;

(4) The present monetary value of the decedent to the persons entitled to receive the damages recovered, including but not limited to compensation for the loss of the reasonably expected

   (a) net income of the decedent,
   (b) services, protection, care, and assistance of the decedent, whether voluntary or obligatory, to the persons entitled to the damages recovered, (c)society, companionship, comfort, guidance, kindly offices, and advice of the decedent to the persons entitled to the damages recovered;
   (c) society, companionship, comfort, guidance, kindly offices, and advice of the decedent to the persons entitled to the damages recovered;

(5) Such punitive damages as the decedent could have recovered had she survived, and the punitive damages for wrongfully causing the death of the decedent through malice, willful or wanton injury, or gross negligence;

(6) Nominal damages when the jury so finds.

15. *Life Expectancy.* In determining the amount of damages to the plaintiff, you may consider how long the plaintiff is likely to live, how long the decedent was likely to have lived, that some persons work all their lives and others do not, that a person's earnings may remain the same or may increase or decrease in the future.

16. *Present Cash Value.* In calculating the amount of damages, you must not simply multiply the life expectancies by the annual damages. Instead, you must determine the present cash value for any award of damages. "Present cash value" means the sum of money needed now, which together with what that sum will earn in the future, will equal the amount of the benefits at the times in the future when they would have been received.

NITA
GENERAL JURY INSTRUCTIONS

The following jury instructions are intended for use with any of the files contained in these materials regardless of whether the trial is in Nita state court or in federal court. In addition, each of the files contains special instructions dealing with the law applicable in the particular case. The instructions set forth here state general principles that may be applicable in any of the cases and may be used at the discretion of the trial judge.[*]

PART I

PRELIMINARY INSTRUCTIONS
GIVEN PRIOR TO THE EVIDENCE
(For Civil or Criminal Cases)

Nita Instruction 01:01 — Introduction

You have been selected as jurors and have taken an oath to well and truly try this cause. This trial will last one day.

During the progress of the trial there will be periods of time when the Court recesses. During those periods of time, you must not talk about this case among yourselves or with anyone else.

During the trial, do not talk to any of the parties, their lawyers or any of the witnesses.

If any attempt is made by anyone to talk to you concerning the matters here under consideration, you should immediately report that fact to the Court.

You should keep an open mind. You should not form or express an opinion during the trial and should reach no conclusion in this case until you have heard all of the evidence, the arguments of counsel, and the final instructions as to the law that will be given to you by the Court.

Nita Instruction 01:02 — Conduct of the Trial

First, the attorneys will have an opportunity to make opening statements. These statements are not evidence and should be considered only as a preview of what the attorneys expect the evidence will be.

---

[*]*The instructions contained in this section are borrowed or adapted from a number of sources including California, Illinois, Indiana, Washington, and Colorado pattern jury instructions.*

Following the opening statements, witnesses will be called to testify. They will be placed under oath and questioned by the attorneys. Documents and other tangible exhibits may also be received as evidence. If an exhibit is given to you to examine, you should examine it carefully, individually, and without any comment.

It is counsel's right and duty to object when testimony or other evidence is being offered that he or she believes is not admissible.

When the Court sustains an objection to a question, the jurors must disregard the question and the answer, if one has been given, and draw no inference from the question or answer or speculate as to what the witness would have said if permitted to answer. Jurors must also disregard evidence stricken from the record.

When the Court sustains an objection to any evidence the jurors must disregard that evidence.

When the Court overrules an objection to any evidence, the jurors must not give that evidence any more weight than if the objection had not been made.

When the evidence is completed, the attorneys will make final statements. These final statements are not evidence but are given to assist you in evaluating the evidence. The attorneys are also permitted to argue in an attempt to persuade you to a particular verdict. You may accept or reject those arguments as you see fit.

Finally, just before you retire to consider your verdict, I will give you further instructions on the law that applies to this case.

PART II

FINAL INSTRUCTIONS
GENERAL PRINCIPLES

General Instructions for Both Civil and Criminal Cases

Nita Instruction 1:01 — Introduction

Members of the jury, the evidence and arguments in this case have been completed, and I will now instruct you as to the law.

The law applicable to this case is stated in these instructions and it is your duty to follow all of them. You must not single out certain instructions and disregard others.

It is your duty to determine the facts, and to determine them only from the evidence in this case. You are to apply the law to the facts and in this way decide the case. You must not be governed or influenced by sympathy or prejudice for or against any party in this case. Your verdict must be based on evidence and not upon speculation, guess, or conjecture.

From time to time the court has ruled on the admissibility of evidence. You must not concern yourselves with the reasons for these rulings. You should disregard questions and exhibits that were withdrawn or to which objections were sustained.

You should also disregard testimony and exhibits that the court has refused or stricken.

The evidence that you should consider consists only of the witnesses' testimonies and the exhibits the court has received.

Any evidence that was received for a limited purpose should not be considered by you for any other purpose.

You should consider all the evidence in the light of your own observations and experiences in life.

Neither by these instructions nor by any ruling or remark that I have made do I mean to indicate any opinion as to the facts or as to what your verdict should be.

Nita Instruction 1:02 — Opening Statements and Closing Arguments

Opening statements are made by the attorneys to acquaint you with the facts they expect to prove. Closing arguments are made by the attorneys to discuss the facts and circumstances in the case, and should be confined to the evidence and to reasonable inferences to be drawn therefrom. Neither opening statements nor closing arguments are evidence, and any statement or argument made by the attorneys that is not based on the evidence should be disregarded.

Nita Instruction 1:03 — Credibility of Witnesses

You are the sole judges of the credibility of the witnesses and of the weight to be given to the testimony of each witness. In determining what credit is to be given any witness, you may take into account his ability and opportunity to observe; his manner and appearance while testifying; any interest, bias, or prejudice he may have; the reasonableness of his testimony considered in the light of all the evidence; and any other factors that bear on the believability and weight of the witness' testimony.

Nita Instruction 1:04 — Expert Witnesses

You have heard evidence in this case from witnesses who testified as experts. The law allows experts to express an opinion on subjects involving their special knowledge, training and skill, experience, or research. While their opinions are allowed to be given, it is entirely within the province of the jury to determine what weight shall be given their testimony. Jurors are not bound by the testimony of experts; their testimony is to be weighed as that of any other witness.

Nita Instruction 1:05 — Direct and Circumstantial Evidence

The law recognizes two kinds of evidence: direct and circumstantial. Direct evidence proves a fact directly; that is, the evidence by itself, if true, establishes the fact. Circumstantial evidence is the proof of facts or circumstances that give rise to a reasonable inference of other facts; that is, circumstantial evidence proves a fact indirectly in that it follows from other facts or circumstances according to common experience and observations in life. An eyewitness is a common example of direct evidence, while human footprints are circumstantial evidence that a person was present.

The law makes no distinction between direct and circumstantial evidence as to the degree or amount of proof required, and each should be considered according to whatever weight or value it may have. All of the evidence should be considered and evaluated by you in arriving at your verdict.

Nita Instruction 1:06 — Concluding Instruction

The Court did not in any way and does not by these instructions give or intimate any opinions as to what has or has not been proven in the case, or as to what are or are not the facts of the case.

No one of these instructions states all of the law applicable, but all of them must be taken, read, and considered together as they are connected with and related to each other as a whole.

You must not be concerned with the wisdom of any rule of law. Regardless of any opinions you may have as to what the law ought to be, it would be a violation of your sworn duty to base a verdict upon any other view of the law than that given in the instructions of the court.

General Instructions for Civil Cases Only

Nita Instruction 2:01 — Burden of Proof

When I say that a party has the burden of proof on any issue, or use the expression "if you find," "if you decide," or "by a preponderance of the evidence," I mean that you must be persuaded from a consideration of all the evidence in the case that the issue in question is more probably true than not true.

Any findings of fact you make must be based on probabilities, not possibilities. It may not be based on surmise, speculation, or conjecture.

Nita Instruction 2:02 — Corporate Party

One (Both) of the parties in this case is a corporation (are corporations), and it is (they are) entitled to the same fair treatment as an individual would be entitled to under like circumstances, and you should decide the case with the same impartiality you would use in deciding a case between individuals.

General Instructions for Criminal Cases Only

Nita Instruction 3:01 — Indictment (Information)

The indictment (information) in this case is the formal method of accusing the defendant of a crime and placing him on trial. It is not any evidence against the defendant and does not create any inference of guilt. The (State) (Government) has the burden of proving beyond a reasonable doubt every essential element of the crime charged in the indictment (information) (or any of the crimes included therein).

Nita Instruction 3:02 — Burden of Proof

The (State) (Government) has the burden of proving the guilt of the defendant beyond a reasonable doubt, and this burden remains on the (State) (Government) throughout the case. The defendant is not required to prove his innocence.

Nita Instruction 3:03 — Reasonable Doubt

Reasonable doubt means a doubt based upon reason and common sense that arises from a fair and rational consideration of all the evidence or lack of evidence in the case. It is a doubt that is not a vague, speculative, or imaginary doubt, but such a doubt as would cause reasonable persons to hesitate to act in matters of importance to themselves.

Nita Instruction 3:04 — Presumption of Innocence

The defendant is presumed to be innocent of the charges against him. This presumption remains with him throughout every stage of the trial and during your deliberations on the verdict. The presumption is not overcome until, from all the evidence in the case, you are convinced beyond a reasonable doubt that the defendant is guilty.

Nita Instruction 3:05 — Reputation/Character

The defendant has introduced evidence of his character and reputation for (truth and veracity) (being a peaceful and law-abiding citizen) (morality) (chastity) (honesty and integrity) (etc.). This evidence may be sufficient when considered with the other evidence in the case to raise a reasonable doubt of the defendant's guilt. However, if from all the evidence in the case you are satisfied beyond a reasonable doubt of the defendant's guilt, then it is your duty to find him guilty, even though he may have a good reputation for _____.

IN THE CIRCUIT COURT OF
DARROW COUNTY, NITA
CIVIL DIVISION

Jeffrey T. Potter,   )
Administrator of the Estate   )
of Katherine Potter, and   )
Jeffrey T. Potter, individually,)
)
        Plaintiff,   )
)
v.   )   JURY VERDICT
)   (Interrogatories)
Charles T. Shrackle and the   )
Shrackle Construction Company,)
)
        Defendants.   )

The jury is to answer the following interrogatories. The foreperson is to answer the interrogatories for the jury and sign the verdict.

Interrogatory No. 1:

Was Charles Shrackle performing duties for or acting on behalf of the Shrackle Construction Company at the time Katherine Potter was struck?

YES _____ NO _____

Interrogatory No. 2:

Please state your findings of negligence in the following form:

We find that the conduct of the defendant, Charles Shrackle, was _____% negligent.

We find that the conduct of the deceased, Katherine Potter, was _____% negligent.

The percentage must total 100%.

Interrogatory No. 3:

Please determine the amount of damages to the plaintiff, Jeffrey Potter, both individually and as administrator of Katherine Potter's estate:

Amount _____$

The percentage of negligence that you find to be apportioned to the defendant, Charles Shrackle (Interrogatory No.2) is multiplied by the amount of damages you determine (Interrogatory No. 3), and that amount will be the verdict for the plaintiff, Jeffrey Potter.

The members of the jury have unanimously answered the interrogatories in the manner that I have indicated.

_____
Foreperson